OILS

OILS

200 TRADITIONAL WAYS WITH NATURE'S OILS IN THE KITCHEN AND HOME, SHOWN IN 350 IMAGES

BRIDGET JONES

southwater

This edition is published by Southwater,
an imprint of Anness Publishing Ltd,
Blaby Road, Wigston,
Leicestershire LE18 4SE;
info@anness.com

www.southwaterbooks.com;
www.annesspublishing.com

If you like the images in this book and would
like to investigate using them for publishing,
promotions or advertising, please visit
our website www.practicalpictures.com
for more information.

Publisher: Joanna Lorenz
Project Editor: Amy Christian
Photography and styling: Michelle Garrett
Additional photography (recipes): Frank Adam,
Edward Allwright, David Armstrong, Tim Auty,
Steve Baxter, Martin Brigdale, Nicki Dowey,
James Duncan, Gus Filgate, Will Heap, Amanda
Heywood, Ferguson Hill, Janine Hosegood,
David Jordan, David King, William Lingwood,
Patrick McLeavey, Thomas Odulate, Craig
Robertson, Gareth Sambridge, Sam Smith, Sam
Stowell, Jon Whitaker.
Recipes: Pepita Aris, Catherine Atkinson, Mridula
Baljekar, Jane Bamforth, Alex Barker, Gillie Başan,
Judy Bastyra, Carla Capalbo, Georgina Campbell,
Miguel de Castro e Silva, Jacqueline Clark, Roz
Denny, Matthew Drennan, Joanna Farrow,
Marina Filippi, Jenni Fleetwood, Christine France,
Silvano Franco, Yasuko Fukuoka, Brian Glover,
Nicola Grimes, Deh-Ta Hsiung, Christine Ingram,
Becky Johnson, Emi Kazuko, Lucy Knox, Vilma
Laus, Lena Lobanov, Kathy Man, Maggie
Mayhew, Jane Milton, Sallie Morris, Keith
Richmond, Rena Salaman, Jennie Shapter, Young
Jin Song, Marlena Spieler, Terry Tan, Liz Trigg,
Christopher Trotter, Linda Tubby, Oona Van Den
Berg, Sunil Vijajakar, Stuart Walton, Biddy White
Lennon, Jenny White, Kate Whitman, Carol
Wilson, Elizabeth Wolf-Cohen, Annette Yates.
Additional projects: Stephanie Donaldson, Jessica
Houdret, Renée Tanner.
Designer: Sarah Rock
Jacket design: Adelle Morris

ETHICAL TRADING POLICY

At Anness Publishing we believe that business
should be conducted in an ethical and
ecologically sustainable way, with respect for
the environment and a proper regard to the
replacement of the natural resources we
employ. As a publisher, we use a lot of wood
pulp in high-quality paper for printing, and that
wood commonly comes from spruce trees. We
are therefore currently growing more than
750,000 trees in three Scottish forest
plantations: Berrymoss (130 hectares/320
acres), West Touxhill (125 hectares/305 acres)
and Deveron Forest (75 hectares/185 acres).
The forests we manage contain more than 3.5
times the number of trees employed each year
in making paper for the books we manufacture.
Because of this ongoing ecological investment
programme, you, as our customer, can have the
pleasure and reassurance of knowing that a tree
is being cultivated on your behalf to naturally
replace the materials used to make the book
you are holding.
Our forestry programme is run in accordance
with the UK Woodland Assurance Scheme
(UKWAS) and will be certified by the
internationally recognized Forest Stewardship
Council (FSC). The FSC is a non-government
organization dedicated to promoting
responsible management of the world's forests.
Certification ensures forests are managed in an
environmentally sustainable and socially
responsible way. For further information about
this scheme, go to
www.annesspublishing.com/trees

© Anness Publishing Ltd 2012

Previously published as part of a larger volume,
Vinegar & Oil

NOTES

Bracketed terms are intended for American readers.
For all recipes, quantities are given in both metric
and imperial measures and, where appropriate, in
standard cups and spoons. Follow one set of
measures, but not a mixture, because they are
not interchangeable.
Standard spoon and cup measures are level.
1 tsp = 5ml, 1 tbsp = 15ml, 1 cup = 250ml/8fl oz.
Australian standard tablespoons are 20ml.
Australian readers should use 3 tsp in place of
1 tbsp for measuring small quantities.
American pints are 16fl oz/2 cups. American
readers should use 20fl oz/2.5 cups in place of
1 pint when measuring liquids.

Electric oven temperatures in this book are for
conventional ovens. When using a fan oven, the
temperature will probably need to be reduced by
about 10–20°C/20–40°F. Since ovens vary, you
should check with your manufacturer's instruction
book for guidance.

The nutritional analysis given for each recipe
is calculated per portion (i.e. serving or item),
unless otherwise stated. If the recipe gives a
range, such as Serves 4–6, then the nutritional
analysis will be for the smaller portion size,
i.e. 6 servings. The analysis does not include
optional ingredients, such as salt added to taste.
Medium (US large) eggs are used unless
otherwise stated.

PUBLISHER'S NOTE

Although the advice and information in this book
are believed to be accurate and true at the time
of going to press, neither the authors nor the
publisher can accept any legal responsibility or
liability for any errors or omissions that may have
been made nor any inaccuracies nor for any loss,
harm or injury that comes about from following
instructions or advice in this book. While every
effort has been made to ensure accuracy when
researching this book, the information on the
therapeutic and cosmetic value of vinegar and oil
is anecdotal and is not intended as a substitute
for the advice of a qualified professional. Any
use to which the recommendations, ideas and
techniques are put is at the reader's sole
discretion and risk. The very young, the elderly,
pregnant women and those in ill-health or with
a compromised immune system are advised
against eating dishes containing raw eggs.

CONTENTS

INTRODUCTION

The far-reaching benefits of oil has been recognized in many different cultures throughout the ages, and its properties mean that it can be used for a huge variety of tasks.

Although nowadays oil is probably most often put to use in the kitchen, it has traditionally filled many roles beyond its food and household purposes, including medicinal and beauty aids and in social and religious rituals. In every aspect of its use, oil enriches whatever it comes in contact with. While it does bring flavours, textures and colours to life, it also creates harmony. This is easy to see in culinary use, where oil enhances dishes or is a valuable rich cooking medium. When oil is combined with other ingredients, it draws the flavours together and has a mellowing effect. It gently highlights some tastes or colours in cooking while subduing others.

Soothing and cleansing

In household use oil-based finishes are applied to bring out the colour and unite the visual features of the wood. The same is true of some metals, where oil acts as a polish and protective layer to help prevent corrosion. Oil is highly regarded as a cleaning material. Instead of harsh chemicals and the

Above: Olive oil is probably the most ancient and widely-used oil in the world.

unwanted films and residues from cans of spray-and-wipe solutions, this natural substance is ideal for restoring fine furniture and for helping to keep the home clean, fresh and eco-friendly.

In the garden oil can also provide quick, easy and environmentally friendly solutions for many simple problems. From pest control to wood preservation, it is increasingly appreciated, and as a natural, non-toxic substance, it is safe to use around children or pets.

Oil has a long-standing reputation for promoting good health and enhancing beauty. Including the many different culinary oils available as part of a balanced diet will contribute to overall well-being and physical health, while externally it provides long-term benefits to the health of skin, hair and nails. Simple preparations can be made at home with store-cupboard items for a fraction of the price of expensive, branded products. With a growing awareness of the need to respect our environment and an increased emphasis on the importance of including unprocessed products in our health and beauty regimes, this is more relevant today than ever.

Kitchen essential

Steeped in history but still vital today, oil has survived advances in food production as well as fashion, not only retaining its place in the household but also increasing in relevance as we learn more about its nutritional properties. It is widely used in the preservation of ingredients to make food items such as sauces, salsas, relishes, bottled or canned salads (antipasti or tapas style) and dressings. Oils extracted from a wide variety of seeds and nuts are readily available from supermarkets, pharmacies, healthfood shops and online.

The chapters in this book offer a glimpse of the history and ancient origins of oil and how it has been put to use over the centuries. A detailed directory outlines the many different types of oil, before practical chapters list the various ways they can be used for health and healing, for natural beauty, around the home, in the garden and of course in the kitchen.

Right: Oil is used as a base for many beauty products, and as an essential lubricant in massage therapies.

AN INTRODUCTION TO OIL

Since ancient times, different oils have been used as a vital source of light, fuel and food, as well as featuring in religious rites and rituals. In today's households a variety of oils still have an important part to play, and are used not only in cooking but for health and diet, in skincare and for wellbeing and indulgence.

Left: Oils are naturally moisturizing and have been used with herbs for skincare since the days of the ancient Egyptian pharaohs.

ANCIENT OIL

From beautifying to embalming, as currency for rulers or chrism for religious leaders, oil has always held physical, social and spiritual significance.

Olive oil was used by the ancient Greeks, Egyptians and Romans, but other oils have been around just as long – nut oils such as groundnut (peanut) oil were used by the Aztecs, while sesame oil was used throughout Asia.

The first production of olive oil

Wall paintings and commercial records show that olives grew in ancient Egypt, and offerings of olive branches – such as those found in the tomb of Tutankhamun – accompanied the dead. The Egyptians used olive oil extensively, for cooking and lighting, in medicine and ritual. They ate the olives they grew, but for the highest quality oil they depended on imports from Palestine, Syria and Crete. The Cretans were producing oil in the third millennium BC and it is possible that this profitable trade was the source of the great wealth of the Minoans.

Above: These giant amphoras from the palace at Knossos were used to store oil.

Above: This 3rd-century Roman mosaic shows men pressing olives to extract oil.

Inhabited during the neolithic period, from the 6th century BC, probably by people who came from Asia Minor, the remains at Knossos on Crete reveal an amazing civilization. A British archaeologist, Arthur Evans, led the excavation of the site in the early 20th century and introduced the term Minoan for the civilization after the ruler King Minos. The discoveries exposed a wealth of information on the architecture, lifestyles and trading of the Minoan civilization, including underground storerooms, jars and vessels that were used for wine and oil. Oil-burning lamps lit the corridors and it was probably one of these that ignited the blaze that finally destroyed the palace. Remains of mills as well as separation tanks and storage vessels provided evidence for the early olive oil production on Crete, from where it was exported to Aegean islands and mainland Greece.

By the 6th century BC, the Greeks had become major exporters of oil, and the olive's status was so high that olive groves were regarded as sacred. In a curious pre-figuring of the modern idea of 'virgin' olive oil, only the chaste were allowed to look after the trees and harvest the crop, and this custom survived into the Middle Ages. At the Panathenaic Games in Athens, held in honour of Athene, the athletes competed for amphorae decorated with paintings of the goddess and filled with olive oil.

Olive oil was vital to the wealth as well as the welfare of ancient Greek and Phoenician civilizations, who traded it and thus spread the appreciation and production from the Eastern Mediterranean through to North Africa, Italy, Spain and Provence in France.

Olive oil was of great importance to the Roman Empire. The Romans ate olives, and developed new methods of curing them, but their greatest contribution to oil production was the invention of the screw press. This enabled them to crush the fruit mechanically to extract the maximum amount of oil from the flesh, but could be set to avoid breaking the stones (pits) and contaminating the oil.

On their travels, the Romans often demanded payment in olive oil. The expansion of the Roman Empire increased the demand for olive oil, and Romans planted trees or traded oil in all the lands they conquered, regarding those who ate animal fats rather than olive oil as barbarians. Olive groves flourished throughout Italy, in southern France and Spain, on all the islands of the Mediterranean and along the north African coast from Tripoli to Algeria.

Other oils

Cultivation of almonds is as ancient as that of olives but the oil is neither as useful nor as significant.

Groundnuts (also known as peanuts or monkey nuts) are another ancient source of oil. These leguminous annual plants were grown in South America from at least 3000–2000BC. The Aztecs were using the nuts as vegetables as well as for making pastes and oils. Groundnut cultivation spread throughout Africa and Asia from the Americas. India, China and the United States of America are now the main producers.

Sesame oil is also ancient in cultivation and use. Unlike the fruits of the aged olive tree, sesame seeds are harvested from an annual plant. Cultivated by the Egyptian Pharaohs, taken from Africa to India, China and Japan, sesame oil was as vital in Asia as olive oil was in the Mediterranean. Sesame oil features in mythology and biblical contexts as a food, for medication and as a beauty product in the same way as olive oil.

Linseed from the flax plant was also known by ancient civilizations. It was used as a food by the Greeks, and Egyptian mummies were bound in linen from the plant. Linseed (or flax) oil was used for culinary purposes, but also as a drying oil in oil painting.

Above: Sesame seeds were first cultivated by the ancient Egyptians.

Rape and soya beans were grown by ancient Chinese civilizations. Rape was also grown in India and soya in Japan. Palm oil comes from trees native to West Africa, producing two types of oil, one from the outer husk of the nut and another from the kernels.

Sunflower seeds have also been used for thousands of years as a source of food. There is evidence to support the cultivation of sunflowers by North American Indians since 900BC. The oil was also used as a hair and skin preparation, and in war paint. In some tribes, Indian mythology included reference to sunflower plants being jealous women who had been turned into plants.

The argan tree is native to Morocco, and oil has been produced from its nuts for thousands of years. Wild Moroccan goats climb the argan trees to feed on the nuts. Traditionally, the Berbers (the indigenous Moroccan people) would collect the undigested stones (pits) of the argan, from the goats' waste underneath the trees. They would grind and press the stones and make a nutty oil that was used in both cooking and for cosmetic purposes.

Above: This oil press was used by the ancient Phoenicians in Tipasa, Algeria.

Above: A hungry goat climbs an argan tree in Morocco to feed on nuts.

OIL THROUGH THE AGES

With worldwide trade, different vegetable oils spread all over the world – including olive oil from Europe, palm oil from West Africa and coconut oil from South-east Asia.

Olive oil is now produced in many different countries, but its use worldwide is relatively small. Production of other oils, namely palm oil and soya oil, is more significant, as they are consumed in much greater quantities.

The spread of olive oil

Olive oil production grew across Europe and beyond. From the 16th century, as the European conquistadors subdued and colonized the New World, olive saplings accompanied missionaries and immigrants on their voyages. Olive cultivation has gradually spread wherever the climate has proved suitable: to California, Chile and Argentina, China, Japan, New Zealand, southern Africa and Australia.

Although olives now grow in many different countries, the Mediterranean still produces most of the world's oil.

Mediterraneans also use the most oil, and consumption is highest of all in Greece, where the average person gets through over 20 litres (35 pints) of olive oil a year.

In recent years, the demand for olive oil has exploded in countries that used to disregard it. In the USA, for instance, consumption rose 2000 per cent between 1980–5, and it continues to increase by about 10 per cent each year. Today there are more than 800 million olive trees, but still about 90 per cent of them grow in their ancient home around the Mediterranean, and many olives are still grown, harvested and processed using techniques that the ancient Greeks and Romans would have recognized.

The production of palm oil

Traditionally produced in West African countries, palm oil was made on large plantations by state-owned slaves.

Above: Oils have been used throughout history for cooking, beauty and health.

Production spread to South-east Asia and Latin America from the 16th century onwards. In Africa, the oil was considered to be so precious that in 1856 in the Kingdom of Dehomey (now the Republic of Benin), a law was passed forbidding the cutting down of oil palms.

During the British Industrial Revolution (in the late 18th and early 19th centuries), palm oil brought back to England by traders was used as an industrial lubricant. It was also used in soap products, such as the Lever Brothers' Sunlight Soap. By the late 1800s, palm oil was the primary export of some West African countries.

Malaysia and Indonesia now produce around 85 per cent of the world's palm oil. Although it is high in saturated fat, which we now know is bad for us, palm oil remains relatively inexpensive, and has a long shelf life,

Above: The olive was, and still is, central to the Italian diet. In the 15th century, Leonardo da Vinci produced sketches for this new and improved olive press.

Above: This painting shows a typical West African palm oil plantation, c. 1845.

and is the most produced and consumed edible oil worldwide. It is used in many developing countries.

Development of other oils

Coconut oil, which is pressed from the flesh of the coconut, was developed as a commercial product by merchants in South Asia in the 19th century. It is very high in saturated fat and not widely used in Western cooking. The Phillipines is the world's largest exporter of coconut oil today.

Spanish explorers probably introduced sunflowers to Europe but it was the Ukraine and Russia that developed sunflower oil to its commercial potential in the early 19th century. In the Ukraine, Alexierka is known as the sunflower capital for its sunflower milling.

Corn oil is a relative newcomer in the oil market. In the early 20th century it was extracted from seeds before they were used for their starch or from the residue in vats after the corn had been fermented for alcohol,

then used for lighting, as a lubricant and in soap production. It was several decades later before it was used as a cooking oil.

The first cottonseed oil was bottled in the USA in the 1880s. A byproduct of the cotton industry, it was used for cooking, but in the 1940s, during World War II, supply could not meet demand, and soya oil was used instead. For several decades, soya oil was the leading vegetable oil in terms of worldwide consumption and production, until palm oil took over. Together, soya oil and palm oil now account for over half of all vegetable oil consumed.

Rapeseed oil had been used in Asia and Europe for centuries, but in the 1970s, Canadian scientists began producing oil from a cultivar of the rapeseed plant. Worried about the negative implication of the name 'rape', they named their oil canola, from the phrase 'Canadian oil, low acid'. Canada is now a major exporter of canola oil.

OIL IN SOAPS

Soaps are produced by a chemical process known as saponification. When a fatty acid reacts with a strong base (alkaline) it produces glycerol and a substance known as the 'salt' of the fatty acid. In relatively simple terms, sodium hydroxide combines with fat to produce a sodium soap – a solid soap. When potassium hydroxide is used a liquid soap is produced. The commercial process includes ingredients for colour, scent and different qualities or uses, such as anti-bacterial properties.

Various vegetable oils are traditionally used in soap making. Olive oil was used for Castile varieties of soap, a term for everyday good-quality 'family' or household soaps. Fancy or toilet soaps were made from palm oil, coconut oil, castor oil or almond oil (lard or tallow, rendered animal fat, especially from cattle and sheep, were also used).

WORLD VEGETABLE OIL CONSUMPTION

Palm oil	31%
Soya oil	29%
Rapeseed (canola) oil	15%
Sunflower oil	8%
Groundnut (peanut) oil	4%
Cottonseed oil	4%
Palm kernel oil	4%
Coconut oil	3%
Olive oil	2%

Source: United States Department of Agriculture (www.usda.gov) 2006

SACRED OIL

From the founding of the city of Athens, to Egyptian goddesses and biblical offerings, oil features in the mythical and religious traditions of many societies.

Oil has been a part of human civilization for thousands of years, and consequently has played a part in many religious rites and rituals.

Oil and ancient mythology

Olive trees were worshipped as sacred in ancient Greece. The tree was said to be a gift to the city of Athens from the goddess Athene. The sacred 'City Olive' tree was planted on the Acropolis.

Olives were traditionally picked and reduced to oil by virgins or pure men. In ancient Greek epic poetry, Homer referred to olive oil as 'liquid gold'. It was used by the gods themselves. In the *Iliad* the goddess Hera uses olive oil as part of a beautifying regime. Aphrodite anoints the body of the Trojan prince Hector with rose-scented olive oil.

In Egyptian legend, Isis was said to have taught man how to cultivate olives. The olive trees were so important that branches were included among the objects placed in the tombs of pharaohs.

In the ancient world, anointing with oil was a general sign of respect for both the living and the dead; guests would be offered oil for their feet on arrival and on leaving.

Oil and religious ritual

The Bible is a very good source of information on the uses of oil, both in society and in a religious context.

Oil was a sign of wealth and olive trees were carefully tended and protected to preserve good fortune. Oil was a currency, used for payment, traded, to meet tithe demands and to

Above: The olive tree, and its oil, feature in ancient Greek mythology.

pay tribute. Throughout the Old and New Testaments, there are references to oil as a food (in bread) and it was also burnt in lamps. Oil was used in ointments for treating the sick, for soothing and healing, as well as for beautification. Honoured guests were anointed with oils on entering a home or before a meal.

The dead were also anointed with oil, a tradition that dated from ancient civilizations who dressed the faces of their deceased with oils to symbolize light and purity, and help them on their way through the underworld.

In religious rituals, oil was, and still is, used in ceremonies to anoint priests during ordination and kings who were enthroned to power. Religious vessels and objects were anointed with oil when they were consecrated. God provided oil for his people and it was withdrawn as a punishment,

Above: Athene's sacred olive tree was planted at the Acropolis in Athens.

Above: Oil has played a part in Christian ceremonies for hundreds of years.

then restored again later. Oil was associated with peace, prosperity, blessings and joy.

Early in the Bible, the significance of the olive tree is established when the dove that Noah sent out from the ark returned bearing a fresh olive leaf as a sign that the waters had subsided and that life could resume. The dove and the olive leaf were a sign of peace.

The Jewish festival of light, Hannukah, celebrates the re-dedication of the temple in Jerusalem. Over the eight days of the festival, an eight-branched candlestick known as a menorah is lit every day to symbolize the oil-burning lamp in the temple that burnt for eight days on sufficient oil for just one day.

The Judaeo-Christian practice of anointing monarchs and priests with oil has its roots in ancient Greek and Roman traditions. The words 'Christ' and 'Messiah' mean 'anointed'.

In Islamic teaching the olive tree is referred to as blessed, neither Eastern nor Western, but providing an oil that glows or shines even without being lit.

Above: The menorah symbolizes the oil-burning lamp that burnt for eight days.

Olive oil was recommended for anointing as well as eating, and it was reputed to cure disease.

Sesame oil, sometimes known as til oil, is considered scared in the Hindu religion. Lamps containing sesame oil are placed in front of statues of the Hindu gods and goddesses as a form of worship.

Above: Oil lamps are placed in front of a statue of Hindu goddess Lakshmi.

Diwali, or the Festival of Lights, is celebrated by Hindus, Sikhs, Buddhists and Jains. During the festival, small lamps called 'diyas' are lit. The diyas consist of a wick inserted into a small clay pot filled with oil, usually coconut oil. The lighting of the diyas represents the triumph of good over evil, knowledge over ignorance and light over dark.

Sacred monuments have traditionally been honoured with oil: libations of oil have been poured over the sacred Omphalos stone at Delphi, the Ka'aba in Mecca and the Jewish Ark of the Covenant. Christian churches are consecrated using holy oil.

HOLY OIL

Olive oil has ancient links with religious rituals. It is used as part of the rituals of anointing but is also burnt in small lamps, to symbolize the process of nourishing the eternal light, providing spiritual nourishment. Just as oil was used to anoint the body of someone who died, candles or lamps lit for the deceased provided a light to lead the way to God.

Above: Libations of oil are used in worship and to consecrate sacred buildings.

FATS: THE FUNDAMENTALS

The right mix of fats, in balanced amounts, promote good health. Limiting the amount of fat we eat is a modern preoccupation, but some fat is an essential part of a balanced diet.

Oils are types of fat. For a healthy balance, we need to know not only how much fat we are eating, but what kind. A little information about what makes liquid and solid fats different, and how they break down in the body, offers insight into how best to use these ingredients.

Fats and oils

Lipid is the general term used for fats and oils. In everyday use, fat usually refers to a solid substance and oil to a liquid. Making a note of the term 'lipid' here is helpful for explaining how fatty foods behave in the body when they are digested, used and eventually passed out of the body.

Chemistry of fats

Fats are triglycerides, made up of fatty acids and glycerol (an alcohol molecule). When digested, lipids are broken down into fatty acids, their building blocks or components. Fatty acids are organic acids that occur naturally in fats and (like other organic substances) they are made up of carbon, hydrogen and oxygen atoms in different proportions. They consist of a chain of carbon and hydrogen atoms with an acid group at one end. Fats are defined by the chemical bonds between their carbon groups.

Saturated and unsaturated fats

Depending on their chemical make-up, the fatty acids can loosely be grouped into saturated or unsaturated. Saturated fatty acids have all the hydrogen atoms they can hold attached to the carbon atoms in the hydrocarbon chain.

Unsaturated fats have some double bonds between the carbon atoms, which means that if these bonds split up into single bonds, another hydrogen atom could attach to take up the spare bond. Unsaturated fats are found in vegetable oils. The unsaturated fatty acids may be polyunsaturated or monounsaturated.

Saturated fatty acids have the maximum number of hydrogen atoms attached, with two to each carbon atom. These have single bonds between the atoms.

Monounsaturated fatty acids do not hold the maximum number of hydrogen atoms but have one double bond.

Polyunsaturated fatty acids hold fewer hydrogen atoms than monounsaturated fatty acids and have more double bonds.

Polyunsaturated fatty acids

The precise arrangement of the atoms can vary in polyunsaturated acids. The usual, natural arrangement of the atoms is termed cis. There is another arrangement of atoms known as trans, familiar from the term trans fatty acids. The trans arrangement does occur naturally in some foods (to some extent in ruminant fats and milk, that is from cud-chewing species, such as sheep and cows) but this is rare and the more common examples of trans arrangement are found in 'unnatural' products, for example produced when polyunsaturated fat is processed by hydrogenation (as in hydrogenated vegetable oil).

Different levels of saturation

Fat in foods is made up of different combinations of fatty acids. Some fats are more saturated than others. Typically, animal fats are thought of as saturated, while vegetable fats are unsaturated, with some being polyunsaturated and others monounsaturated. Foods can be said to be 'high in saturated fats' or 'rich in monounsaturated fats', indicating the balance of saturated to unsaturated fatty acids in the structure as a whole.

Solid or liquid fats

Saturated fats tend to be solid at room temperature while unsaturated fats are liquid. Butter, lard and meat dripping set at room temperature and become firm when chilled. They have to be heated to melt. By comparison, unsaturated vegetable oils are liquid at room temperature. Place olive oil in a very cold

Above: Vegetable oils are liquid at room temperature, whereas animal fats such as lard or butter are solid.

place in the refrigerator and it will thicken but it will not set. Some animal fats are less saturated than others: for example, poultry fat is softer than meat dripping; pork fat is less solid than lamb or beef fat. There are a few exceptions to the animal-vegetable rule: for example, coconut oil and palm kernel oil have high levels of saturated fat. Unsaturated fats that are usually liquid can be processed to make them more saturated and less liquid. Techniques for processing oils so that they are set at room temperature are used to make margarine and spreads. One of the processes is hydrogenation.

Hydrogenation and trans fatty acids

The process of hydrogenation involves pumping hydrogen atoms through the fat at pressure. The available double bonds may then take on some of the hydrogen atoms to become more saturated. Instead of the natural cis arrangement, they may form a trans arrangement, and this results in production of trans fatty acids.

The problem with trans fatty acids is that there is evidence to support links between a high dietary intake and disease; in other words, they may have adverse effects on health, for example, they have been associated with cardiovascular disease and high levels of blood cholesterol.

Hydrogenation was introduced to the manufacture of culinary fats early in the 20th century when margarine was in the process of development. The process is referred to as hardening and it is used for vegetable oils and fish oils in some mass-produced, processed products. As well as margarine, hydrogenated oils are used as cooking fats and are listed among the ingredients on a wide range of products, from spreads, sauces and dressings; biscuits and cookies; pies, pastries and baked goods to hot drink powder mixes.

Above: It is important to include some fats in your diet to achieve the right balance.

Above: Monounsaturated fatty acids can be found in olive oil.

Above: Sunflower oil contains high levels of polyunsaturated fatty acids.

Food manufacturers and retailers are aware of the possible negative effects of a diet high in trans fatty acids. As a result, the widespread use of hydrogenated oils in some cases has, and in many cases still is, being addressed. While some retailers have publicized the fact that they have banned the use of hydrogenated oils and fats in their own-brand products, this is not universal. Check food labels for hydrogenated oils and the ingredients list may come as a surprise. Avoid them where possible and use alternatives.

Essential fatty acids

The body can manufacture the majority of the fatty acids it needs with the exception of two that have to be included in the diet. These are the polyunsaturated alpha-linolenic acid and linoleic acid. Three other important polyunsaturated fatty acids include eicosapentaenoic acid (EPA) and docosahexaenoic acid (DHA) that can be manufactured from alpha-linolenic acid, and arachidonic acid that can be formed from linoleic acid.

Above: Walnuts and their oil are rich in essential omega-3 fatty acids.

Omega-3 and omega-6 fatty acids

The terms omega-3 and omega-6 refer to the type of chemical structure and the position of the double bonds. Alpha-linolenic acid, EPA and DHA are part of the omega-3 group of fatty acids and linoleic acid is one of the omega-6 fatty acids. Omega-3 fatty acids are found in fish oils and some vegetable oils, including walnut, flax seed (linseed) and rapeseed (canola) oils. Omega-6 fatty acids are found in nuts and seeds, and their oils.

Lipoproteins and cholesterol

Fats and fatty acids are not water soluble. In the body, the blood is the transport system for nutrients that have been digested from food. So that digested fats can be carried around in the blood and taken to the cells where they are needed, they have protein molecules (produced in the liver and intestine) attached to them. This produces lipoproteins – the fats (lipids) with protein attached.

There are different types of lipoproteins designed for different functions but their fundamental role is to act as carriers, taking the lipids to the cells where they are needed. There are chylomicrons, high-density lipoproteins (HDL), low-density lipoproteins (LDL) and very low-density lipoproteins.

Potentially 'negative' fats

The LDLs carry about three-quarters of the cholesterol in the blood, taking it to the cells where it is required. When there is an excess of LDLs (more than needed for use in the cells), the cholesterol carried is deposited on the smooth muscle wall of the blood vessels. The LDLs are often referred to as bad fats.

This can lead to a build-up of plaque on the insides of the arteries, which slowly reduces the space for blood flow, which in turn increases the pressure. It is bad news for the body, leading to

Above: Check the labels carefully when buying oils – avoid hydrogenated oils.

increased blood pressure, strain on the heart and cardiovascular disease. Eventually, the vessels may block up completely or bits of plaque may break off and cause a blockage.

Potentially 'positive' fats

HDLs are the carriers that work in the opposite direction. They are responsible for removal of excess cholesterol from the blood, taking it back to the liver where it can be processed and removed from the system. Including a good level of HDLs in the diet helps to control blood cholesterol; they are often referred to as 'good' fats.

Sources of cholesterol

Some cholesterol is obtained from food but the majority is produced by the liver. Even if the diet is not high in cholesterol, the body may manufacture it. There may be some natural disposition to produce more cholesterol – something genetic that means the level of cholesterol is higher than desirable. Having a diet rich in LDLs and low in HDLs will contribute to raised blood cholesterol, but some people who have relatively low-fat diets and are not overweight can still have raised blood cholesterol levels. Eating good fats, maintaining a healthy weight and exercise can help.

Antioxidants

Fat soluble vitamin E is a particularly useful antioxidant, so eating good fats in the right proportion helps to provide antioxidants as well as carriers for taking away excess cholesterol. Fruit and vegetables are also rich in antioxidants, including vitamin C and betacarotene.

Rancidity

The term for fats and oils that have gone off due to oxidation or hydrolysis, and have an unpleasant flavour and odour is 'rancid'. Some fats are more prone to rancidity than others.

Oxidation takes place when fats are exposed to air and the process speeds up in warm, light conditions. Unsaturated fats are more prone to oxidation than saturated fats. This is also one of the reactions that influences the freezer life of foods and some fats become rancid during freezing relatively quickly, especially when salted and/or poorly wrapped with inadequate packing. Bacon is a good example as it will become rancid quickly when frozen.

Oils that are left in half-filled, unsealed bottles will become rancid quickly, especially when left in sunlight. Oil and vinegar bottles should not be left for table use over days or weeks. The salad oil will soon deteriorate and become rancid.

Hydrolysis is a reaction promoted or speeded up by air-borne bacteria, typically in butter that is left uncovered at room temperature. Butter is made up of a certain proportion of water as well as fat. Unlike oxidation, hydrolysis is a reaction between water and fat, with both being broken down. Ghee or clarified butter is heated gently until all the water evaporates, then the salt content and other solids are strained off, leaving a pure fat that does not become rancid easily. Clarified butter is as stable as some oils and more so than others.

Above: Oil that is left out on the table in an unsealed bottle will soon become rancid and unusable. Instead, bottles should be sealed and stored in a cool, dark place.

OILS AND FREE RADICALS

One of the associations between free radicals and fats is in heating. When fats are heated to very high temperatures they begin to break down and form free radicals. Sometimes, it is not one-off heating to a high temperature that causes the problem, but repeated heating, for example when deep-frying in the same fat several times over. Gradually the fat breaks down and develops off flavours.

Just as some fats are solid (butter) and others are liquid (oil), some can be heated to a higher temperature than others before they begin to break down, develop a nasty smell, bitter flavour and burn. This is called the smoking point, when the fat begins to give off a smoke and smell acrid. Some oils break down at lower temperatures than others, making them less suitable for cooking. Not only does the flavour of the oil change but the nutritional value is reduced and free radicals are formed. Overheating oils is not recommended and some oils are best reserved for cold preparation.

The smoking point is lowered each time the oil is heated or used for cooking, as some breakdown occurs at moderate temperatures. Frying in the same oil over and over also leads to breakdown, bad flavours and free radical production. If oil is used more than once, it should be strained to remove bits of leftover food that will overheat and burn with repeated frying.

Vegetable oils reach smoking point at different temperatures. Oils which are unrefined often have a lower smoking point than refined oils. This makes them unsuitable for cooking methods requiring high temperatures, such as deep-frying.

OIL PRODUCTION

The Romans invented a screw press to extract oil from olives many centuries ago. Since then, technologies have advanced, but the basic principles of oil production have not altered.

When oil is made, the basic ingredient – seeds, nuts or fruit – from which the oils are taken undergoes a series of different stages of production. The precise method is important for the quality of the oil. The ingredients are cleaned, milled and pressed to extract the oil, which is then allowed to settle, and is filtered or processed to remove unwanted water and debris. Technology has taken over for mass production but some artisan products are still produced following old-fashioned methods.

Traditional oil extraction

The first stages of oil production involve separating the seeds or fruit from the unwanted debris, such as stems, twigs and leaves, and then washing the basic product if

Above: This 15th-century engraving shows the production methods that were commonly used to make Italian olive oil in the 1600s. The olives are crushed by a stone press.

Above: Wooden presses were originally used to extract the oil from olives.

necessary, for example when processing olives or avocados. Seeds and nuts have to be hulled or shelled.

Traditional methods of production for olives involved crushing the ingredients to a paste by hand and mixing the paste to warm it and help release the oil. The paste was then spread on mats, stacked and pressed to extract the oil and all the juices. When the paste was allowed to stand, the oil would float on top of the water-soluble juices. It would then be separated.

Modern oil production

The basic principles used in oil production today remain the same but the technology has advanced.

Crushing can be done by steel rollers or tooth grinders rather than using stones. Malaxation, the process of mixing, is controlled to allow a certain level of natural heating (27–8°C) but not too much. The higher the temperature and the longer the mixing time, the greater the yield of oil will be. The liquid oil mixture is then separated from the solids, known as the pomace. Instead of standing it in tanks to allow the oil to surface and separate, a centrifuge is used to speed up the process. Centrifugation involves spinning at high speed so that the oil is separated from the solids and other juices. Centrifugation may be used instead of pressing in some processes.

Depending on the type of equipment and techniques used, the oil may be filtered under carefully controlled conditions to remove bits of pulp and shell, sometimes referred to as foots. Further processing may be necessary for some oils, including, for example, refining, bleaching and deodorizing.

Cold or hot pressing

For cold pressing of oil the basic ingredients are not heated before they are ground. The process does not extract the maximum amount of oil and the remaining oil, in the form of a 'cake', can be further processed. Cold pressed oils are not refined but they are filtered. The yield is far lower but premium oil is produced, with fuller flavour and greater nutrient retention. Some cold pressed oils have a sediment that may be retained for its flavour. The residue oil in the cake from the first cold pressing can then be extracted by hot pressing, resulting in inferior oil.

For hot pressing, the ingredients may be heated before crushing or alternatively the crushed paste may itself be heated, for example by steaming or roasting. This helps the cells to break down and release oil but the heating also releases other constituents of the basic ingredients. The oils have to be further processed to remove unwanted substances that have been released by heating.

Some processes involve adding solvents for maximum extraction, resulting in a product from which the oil has to be separated from the solvent mix by further heating.

Traditional classification of oils

Oils were traditionally classified by several criteria, such as origins, properties and uses. The categories of animal, vegetable and mineral oils covers fish oils, the familiar edible vegetable oils and types of fuel oil respectively. Another means of

Above: The types of olive oil can be recognized by colour; cold pressed olive oil has a distinctive green shade.

grouping oils is by their chemical properties, either fixed or volatile. While fixed oils do not rapidly evaporate (or do not evaporate at all), volatile oils evaporate comparatively quickly and these include the essential oils now familiar for aromatherapy.

Oils can be referred to as 'drying' or 'non-drying', terms that will be familiar to artists who use oil-based painting media. Drying oils are also a key component of many varnishes. When drying oils are exposed to air, they form a tough surface. A good example is boiled linseed oil, which is excellent as a wood preservative; this is inedible due to the metallic dryers that are used in its production. Boiled linseed oil is thicker than the normal oil and has a shorter drying time. Ordinary linseed oil does not have the same properties and will not dry as quickly – it will remain sticky when applied in quantities that cannot be soaked up. Other commonly used drying oils include tung oil, poppy seed oil and walnut oil.

Above: Bottles are filled with oil on a production line in a modern oil factory.

DIRECTORY OF OILS

There is an amazing variety of oils suitable for all sorts of applications, from frying food to beautifying the complexion, and from the well-known Mediterranean olive oil, to Moroccan argan oil and South-east Asian coconut oil. Many familiar, relatively inexpensive oils can work their magic beyond the kitchen, using methods that have been passed down through many generations. This section provides a guide to oils that are readily available for household use – from cooking and cleaning, to relaxing and reviving.

Left: Vegetable oils vary in colour, from very pale, almost colourless yellows to rich browns.

A WIDE RANGE OF OILS

Many different oils are now available to the modern consumer. It is important to know how to choose the right oils, as well as to store them correctly and eventually dispose of them safely.

Many types of edible oils are used all over the world. Historically, different countries have used oils pressed from whatever raw material was available to them. Olive oil has been used in the Mediterranean for centuries, while palm oil is popular in Africa, Asia and South America.

Some oils are used specifically for their flavour. Sesame oil and groundnut (peanut) oil are used in Asian cooking, for example in stir-fried dishes, to impart a nutty flavour. Other oils, such as grape seed oil, are favoured for their very mild flavour.

Other edible oils which are available include coconut (or copra) oil, soya oil, sunflower oil, rice bran oil, safflower oil, corn (or maize) oil, flax (or linseed) oil, wheatgerm oil, avocado oil, pumpkin seed oil, hemp seed oil and poppy seed oil. Some oils are more common than others, although most can be sourced from specialist and online retailers.

Vegetable oil

Cooking oils which are sold simply with the label 'vegetable oil' are usually a blend of a variety of oils such as sunflower, corn or soya oil. The exact contents of the oil will be listed on the bottle.

Not all vegetable oils are edible. Examples of such oils include processed linseed oil and tung oil. These oils can be put to use around the house, outside of the kitchen.

Buying oils

The majority of larger supermarkets sell a good selection of oils, from basic vegetable cooking oil, through various seed and nut oils to an increasingly broad variety of olive oils. Larger supermarkets usually have a good stock turnover but some of the expensive less-common oils may have been stored for rather longer than ideal in a warm light environment. Healthfood shops and delicatessens usually offer a different selection, often including the more unusual oils; buy from busy shops to ensure that the stock is not old.

Storing oil

Oil becomes rancid when stored in a warm, light place for any length of time. Dark, airtight bottles are the best containers. Buy oil in quantities that will be used fairly quickly, especially the more expensive types, such as nut oils, that are unlikely to be used as extensively. Make space in a cool cupboard, for example, well

TASTING OILS

By assembling a number of distinctive oils you can try a comparative tasting of oils in the same way as you would taste wine. It may be interesting to try several varieties of the same oil, for example olive oil, of which there are many types available to buy.

Pour each oil into a small glass. Warm the oil in your hands and swirl it around the glass, then inhale to test the aroma. Take a small sip and note the flavours, which for olive oil can range from fruity, mellow or grassy to peppery and pleasantly bitter. The oil should not taste fatty in the mouth, or acidic in the throat. Cleanse your palate between oils by eating a slice of apple.

Above: Taste small amounts of different oils and compare flavours and aromas.

Above: Warm oil in your hands before tasting it, to release the flavour.

away from cooking appliances, washing machine or tumble dryer, refrigerator or freezer (they give out quite a lot of heat). A cupboard on an external wall is usually cooler.

Oils can be stored in the refrigerator if there is no cool cupboard in the kitchen but as space can be a problem, limit this for best olive oils or other oils that may not be used on an everyday basis.

It is pointless having a wide variety of 'treat' oils that are used infrequently, only to discover that they have gone off when the bottles are half empty. It is better to decide on one or two good oils for frequent use and have phases for one or two 'special' oils, buying small bottles to use fairly quickly.

Check the storage instructions and use-by dates on individual bottles because oils vary in their processing, which in turn influences their keeping quality.

Special care should be taken when storing oils that have been flavoured with herbs or other ingredients. Flavoured oil should always be strained; if remnants of the herb remain in the oil, harmful bacteria can develop.

Disposal of oil

Oil that has been used for cooking, for example after deep-frying, should not be poured down the sink as it can cause blockages in pipes. Instead, it should be allowed to cool, then transferred to a suitable container, sealed and disposed of with other household waste. This is not very environmentally friendly, however, and there are alternatives. Recycling schemes for cooking oil exist in some areas, and small amounts of vegetable oil may be safely added to a compost heap.

Above: Sesame oil has a distinctive flavour and is commonly used in Eastern cooking.

Above: Olive oil is widely used in many traditional Italian dishes.

Above (clockwise from top): Pumpkin seed oil, hazelnut oil, grape seed oil and corn oil.

OLIVE OIL

Centuries old, olive oil is widely used for culinary and other products, from the best dining to candles and the finest soaps and beauty products.

Used regularly in the ancient world, olive oil, along with bread and wine, is one of the oldest foods in existence. Away from the Mediterranean climate, animal fats were historically favoured as cooking fats until relatively recently. Its popularity has now grown worldwide, and today olive oil is the oil for which there is the most variety and choice available.

Much has been written about the history, extraction, types and uses of olive oil. Tree, olives and oil feature throughout the history of the ancient world, and olive oil continues to be a source of research and development. The global food market has evolved such that oil aficionados may sample the products not only of different countries but of specific producers and from the fruit of identified varieties. In the past, simply using virgin olive oil was indicative of culinary sophistication. Nowadays the average supermarket offers a choice of at least a few different types of olive oil while larger outlets display shelves of olive oils from many different countries. The following background information provides a starting point for exploring the nuances of the many olive oils that are now available.

Places and production

The Mediterranean countries are still the focus for olive cultivation. Spain, Italy and Greece are key producers of olive oil. Turkey, Syria, Tunisia, Morocco, Portugal, France and California contribute, as do Australia and South Africa to a far lesser extent. Producing countries export their olives and oil but they also import olive oil; for example, Italy is the second largest producer in the world, but the Italians themselves consume more oil than they produce – 11 litres (19 pints) per person each year – and Italian law allows the producers to import oil for blending and bottling without stating its original source. So, while some of the finest single estate oils come from Italy, most of the blended oil labelled 'bottled in Italy' on the supermarket shelf is actually Spanish, Greek or Tunisian in origin. Consumption per person is significantly higher in Greece than in either Spain or Italy.

Olive varieties

There are many varieties of *Olea Europaea*, the cultivated olive tree, with national and regional names. Greece is known for its Koroneiko and Kalamata olives. From Spain, Picual, Hojiblanca and Verdial olives are popular in Andalusia;

Above: Olive oil has been part of the Mediterranean diet for thousands of years.

Above: With its renowned health-giving qualities, olive oil is now used worldwide.

Above: There are many varieties of olive, each producing different types of oil.

Above: Olives that have been hand-picked will be used to make the finest and most expensive olive oils.

Above: Olives in higher branches are picked using a small rake. The olives bruise easily so great care must be taken.

Above: Large nets are placed on the ground around the trees in order to catch the olives as they fall.

further north, Cornicabra olives are the focus of Castilla La Mancha; while in the Aragon and La Rioja regions, the Arbequina and Empeltre olives dominate.

Italy is well known for its regional oils with their separate characteristics resulting from the different soil types and weather patterns. Tuscany is the major area for olive oil production and one of the major exporters to other regions. Italy provides oils with all types of characteristics, from the light and fruity to robust and spicy. Moraiolo, Frantoio, Leccino and Pendolino are among the main varieties of olive grown.

Quality and flavour

The flavour of the olive oil depends on a number of contributing factors. The variety of olives and the conditions under which they are grown obviously influence the characteristics of the oil. Just as in wine production, the type of soil and weather also play their part. The skills of the producer in planting and caring for the trees as well as in judging the

harvest and the ripeness of the olives are also extremely important for the quality of the oil.

Traditional planting allows about 32 trees to the acre. Left to grow, the trees can reach a height of 10–15m (30–50 feet), living for up to a thousand years. Careful pruning and feeding are necessary to prevent the tree from growing to full height while preserving the fruit-bearing branches that yield a good crop for practical harvesting. Pest control involves preventing insect and fungal attacks that are typical of all tree nurturing, but the olive moth is the particular pest that will consume the leaves and buds.

Harvesting and processing

The olives have to be ripe but not too ripe to produce good oil, and the way in which they are handled influences the finished product. The harvesting season varies according to the region and conditions but typically takes place between November and February.

Harvesting methods and production techniques should be as gentle as possible for producing the finest oils. Protecting the olives against damage is important to help prevent the flesh from deteriorating in quality between picking and processing. Hand-picking is still practised for the finest oils. Producers who go to these lengths will use the fact that the oil is extracted from hand-picked olives as a major selling point. Other methods include netting the ground under the trees to catch the fruit as the trees are shaken or when the olives drop naturally, as hitting the ground causes bruising.

The olives are loaded into baskets and taken for cleaning, sorting and extraction. The time lapse influences the quality of the oil and alters the acidity of the olives, which naturally begin to ferment once they are picked. While a short period of storage may improve the end product, too long will spoil it and allow off flavours to develop. The olives may be taken to a central processing plant or the grower may also have the necessary processing equipment.

Grades of olive oil

Olive oil is graded according to its acidity levels as well as the quality of the flavour and aroma. Extra virgin and virgin olive oils are from the first pressing, are produced by cold pressing and do not contain any refined olive oil.

Extra virgin olive oil has a maximum acidity of 0.8% (according to IOOC standards) or 1% by some regulations. The oil must have a good flavour and odour.

Virgin olive oil must have good flavour and odour, with maximum acidity of 2%.

Ordinary virgin olive oil has a maximum acidity of 3% but the flavour is generally not as good as the superior types.

Refined olive oil is a term that may be used for oil obtained from virgin live oils by refining methods that do not alter the structure of the oil. Refined olive oil has a very low acidity level, for example as low as 0.2%.

Pure olive oil or olive oil is oil that contains a blend of refined and virgin olive oils. They generally have a maximum acidity of 1.5%. These oils do not have the full flavour or range of flavours of the extra virgin or virgin oils.

Lampante is the term for oil with an acidity level higher than 3.3%, poor flavour and unpleasant aroma. This type of oil is not suitable for consumption but can be used for non-food use. It can be refined, bleached and deodorized to produce an edible oil that can be blended with better quality oils. Alternatively, the refined oil may be used in food processing or for packing (for example, when olive oil is used in the canning industry).

Manufacturer's terms

Apart from the formal grading, other terms and names are used on labels.

Light olive oil or mild olive oil are terms for refined olive oils, meaning that they are bland in flavour. Light olive oil may be used in blended oil products, for example, where olive and sunflower oils are mixed, and this will be stated on the label. 'Light' or 'lite' does not refer to the fat content of the oil.

Blended olive oil indicates that the oil is made up of oils from different varieties of olive and different regions. Blending is used to maintain a consistent standard. When the term applies to a mixture of oils, the other types of oil (sunflower or rapeseed oil, for example) must be listed.

Early or late harvest oils refer to the ripeness of the olives from which the oil has been extracted. The flavours will be quite different if fully ripe olives are used compared to green olives.

Unfiltered oil will retain some of the paste, which is thought to give more flavour, and produce a sediment.

Cold pressed oil

In regulation terms, cold pressed refers to the maximum temperature of 27°C/80°F that the olive paste may reach during the mixing process.

Above: Modern production lines allow oil to be produced on a much greater scale to meet the growing demand.

Above: Strict rules govern the grading of olive oil, set by the International Olive Oil Council in Madrid.

Above: Kalamata olives after the first pressing with traditional stone rollers, still used in oil presses in Greece.

Above: Olive oil was used as a moisturizer by the ancient Romans, and still makes a quick and easy treatment for dry skin.

Above: Traditional olive oil soap, or 'savon de Marseille', has been manufactured in France for hundreds of years.

Above: Inexpensive olive oil can be used around the house as a natural cleaner, restorer and furniture polish.

The paste warms naturally during mixing, increasing with the length of mixing; applying a maximum temperature controls the quality of the oil. Increasing the temperature gives a higher yield but the flavour is inferior.

Flavour characteristics

The flavours of different olive oils vary significantly and many of the terms used to describe the analysis of the oils resemble those used in wine tasting.

Oils may be 'robust', 'fruity' and 'full flavoured', especially when extracted from olives that are just about ripe. Full fruity flavours are positive. Lighter flavours may include hints of 'green' or slightly 'grassy' tones and these may be positive, combined with lighter fruit flavours, such as apple. 'Sweet' is used when the oil does not have sharp or bitter qualities to its flavour. This term does not mean sweet in sugary terms but by comparison to sharp. The words 'spicy' or 'peppery' are used to describe complex flavours reminiscent of sweet spices or of slightly hotter pepper.

Sometimes olive oils are criticized for poorly balanced flavour or for unwelcome characteristics that may include bitterness or earthy tones. Cucumber-like flavours are not good and may indicate that the oil has been stored for too long (but has not been exposed to air or high heat, so has not gone rancid). Some oils may be described as 'harsh', 'astringent' or 'rough'.

USE

- In all aspects of cookery: as a cooking medium, for stir-frying, as an ingredient in baking, for marinades, sauces and dressings, in dips with other ingredients.
- To make your own herb- or spice-flavoured oils.
- As a simple dip on its own to moisten good bread.
- As a beauty product. Olive oil is a traditional hair and skin conditioner.
- As a health supplement.
- To restore, clean and polish woods, metals or leather.
- As a lubricant for stiff locks and hinges.

SETTING STANDARDS

The International Olive Oil Council (IOOC) based in Madrid, Spain, is responsible for the standards that are applied, terms, descriptions and the labelling of different oils.

Founded in 1956, following the first International Olive Oil Agreement, the original aims of the organization were to modernize and promote the growing of olives and olive products and to draw up international procedures for the sector. The United States has its own set of rules for olive oil producers but there is some pressure for producers there to follow the IOOC guidelines.

NUT OILS

Strongly flavoured, rich in vitamin E and with high levels of monounsaturated fat, versatile nut oils are a great addition to any store cupboard.

Almond oil

Along with olive trees, almond trees have been cultivated since ancient times in the Mediterranean basin, but with the emphasis on the nuts themselves rather than for oil extraction. Almonds are still grown across the Mediterranean. California is one of the world's major growing areas, as are Italy and Spain. Almonds contain 40 to 60 per cent oil.

There are two types of almond oil extracted from different botanical species. Sweet almond oil has a mild taste, while bitter almond oil has the distinctive, strong almond flavour. **Sweet almond oil** is light and flavourless. Although it can be used as a cooking medium for food, it is quite expensive. It is usually

Above: Almonds have been cultivated for thousands of years. Oil extraction only forms a small part of their use.

used in baking, as a final dressing for hot foods, as a base for salad dressings, or in sweet dishes where a distinct flavour is not required. It is useful for greasing moulds for setting cold dishes, especially sweet foods. Away from the kitchen, sweet almond oil is widely used as a base oil for massage and aromatherapy uses. Being light and odourless, it makes a good carrier for the aromatic essential oils.

USE
- In sweet baking mixtures, such as American muffins and cookies.
- To drizzle over food, such as salads or charcuterie, to moisten it and introduce a hint of oil without additional flavour.
- As a base for light salad dressings.
- As a carrier oil in aromatherapy.

Bitter almond oil In nature, bitter almonds contain a substance known as amygdalin that can produce the toxin prussic acid or hydrogen cyanide. In processing the bitter almonds, the prussic acid is eliminated, making the oil safe for culinary use. Bitter almond oil is used in very small quantities as a flavouring in sweet cooking, including baking and confectionery.

USE
- As a flavouring ingredient in sweet baking, blancmange or desserts.

Almond oil with flavouring In addition to the two oils, some almond oils are based on sweet almond oil with

Above: Sweet almond oil is expensive and is not widely used in cooking. It is often used in aromatherapy as a carrier oil

flavouring added, to produce an oil with a light almond flavour. This can be used to make dressings with a light almond flavour or drizzled over a variety of savoury or sweet foods.

Groundnut (peanut) oil

Peanuts, groundnuts or monkey nuts are popular for a wide variety of culinary uses across Asia, Africa and South America. They have long been used in cooking and as a source of oil.

Groundnut oils may be cold pressed, in which case they retain the distinct flavour of the nut, or refined to produce a light oil that is virtually flavourless. The refined oil is ideal for deep-frying as it has a high smoking point, therefore it can be heated to a high temperature. The cold pressed oil

Above: Groundnut oil is often used in Asian cooking, such as stir-fries.

Above: The sweet flavour of hazelnut oil makes it ideal for use in desserts.

Above: Walnut oil is rich in vitamin E and is perfect for use in salad dressings.

can also be used as a cooking medium in dishes that benefit from its flavour, but it cannot be heated to the same high temperature so is not suitable for deep-frying. Both types of oil can be used for roasting, baking, shallow frying, stir-frying, or in sauces and dressings, including mayonnaise.

Butterine oil was an old-fashioned term for the oil obtained from a second cold pressing of groundnut oil, and this was used as an edible oil as well as a fuel. (Butterine was also a name applied to margarine.) Hot pressed oil from a further processing was used in the soap-making industry. Groundnut oil was often used to adulterate olive oil and lard. In turn, it was adulterated by the addition of cotton seed oil, poppy seed oil and rapeseed (canola) oil.

USE
- Refined or cold pressed groundnut oil for speedy stir-frying (the former is preferable when cooking at very high temperatures).
- As part of a coating or to brush food before baking or grilling (broiling).

- In salsas, dressings, dips and sauces, such as satay dipping sauce, for a distinct peanut flavour.
- Refined oil for deep-frying to give crisp, dry results.
- As a base oil for massage.

Hazelnut oil

This has the distinct flavour of the nuts and is excellent for drizzling over a wide variety of hot or cold foods as a dressing. It can be used in either savoury or sweet dishes. Hazelnut oils are produced in Turkey, Greece, Italy and Spain as well as in the United States. It is valued primarily for its nutty flavour.

USE
- To drizzle the oil over leafy salads, cheese, meat and poultry as a dressing.
- On its own or mixed with a lighter oil in salad dressings.
- In light dips and to finish creamy sauces for flavour.
- In sweet creams and with syrups or honey to make dessert sauces.
- As a carrier oil for massage.

Walnut oil

Growing wild across Asia and the Balkan countries, walnut trees were probably first cultivated in Turkey and Iran. The trees are now cultivated in many countries all over the world, from Russia, East Asia and across the Mediterranean countries to France, where there is a long history of cultivation and oil production. California is now the major producer.

Walnuts contain about 70 per cent fat, with a high percentage of monounsaturated fatty acids. They are also a good source of vitamin E. Walnut oil is expensive and used for its flavour rather than as a cooking medium.

USE
- To drizzle over foods, savoury or sweet, in dressings and sauces for hot or cold dishes.
- In marinades and dressing for cooked meats, cheese or fruit.
- In savoury dips or sweet creams, syrups or sauces.
- To flavour sweet dishes, moisten cakes or pastries.
- As a base oil for massage.

Pistachio nut oil

The pistachio tree is native to the Middle East, Asia and India where it has grown wild for centuries. It was probably first cultivated in Asia and introduced to Europe by the Romans, then on to America. The nuts contain up to about 55 per cent oil, of which 50 per cent is monounsaturated. The nuts are valued as an ingredient in savoury cooking, with oil extraction being relatively unimportant. The oil is well flavoured and expensive, and most suitable for use as a dressing or for final flavouring in savoury and sweet cooking.

USE

- To drizzle over cooked foods, cheese or salads.
- In dressings, sauces and dips.
- To flavour sweet dishes, creams and syrups.

Macadamia nut oil

Also known as Queensland nuts, macadamia nuts originated in Australia, where they are a traditional

Above: Pistachio nut oil varies in colour, depending on production methods, from a distinctive green to a paler yellow.

Aboriginal food. They were introduced to Hawaii in the late 19th century and they are also cultivated in South America and Africa. The nuts are widely valued for their flavour and texture. They are rich in vitamin E and monounsaturated oil and contain about 70 per cent fat.

Above: Pistachio nuts are generally valued more for use in cooking than for the expensive oil extracted from them.

These expensive nuts yield an equally expensive oil (only a small percentage of the nuts are designated for oil extraction) that is light coloured and textured, with the distinct yet delicate flavour of macadamia nuts. Although light, there is a certain rich, creaminess to the flavour.

Macadamia nuts are used in commercial bakery and confectionery products and the oil is valued in the cosmetics industry. It is reputed to have excellent moisturizing and antioxidant qualities that are valuable in products for skincare.

USE

- As a dressing, drizzled over cheeses and cooked foods.
- In salad dressings.
- To flavour and enrich sauces and dips.
- With chocolate and sweet ingredients for making rich sauces and dressings for desserts, ice creams and cakes.
- In natural skincare remedies.

Above: Macadamia nuts are processed ready for oil extraction.

Above: Macadamia nuts are expensive, and as a result so is their oil.

OTHER EDIBLE VEGETABLE OILS

There is now a huge variety of edible vegetable oils available to us – from the less familiar African palm oil and coconut oil to store-cupboard staples such as sunflower and corn oil.

Palm oil

A native of Africa, cultivation of the oil palm has spread to Asia and South America, and it is one of the richest sources of oil on the planet. There are two distinct types of palm oil and it is important to differentiate between them. *Palm oil* is the term for oil that is extracted from the fibrous pulp of the fruit, which contains about 50 per cent fat. This oil contains about 50 per cent saturated fatty acids and about 40 per cent monounsaturated fatty acids with about 10 per cent polyunsaturated fatty acids. The oil is strongly coloured red or orange due to its high betacarotene content. The oil also provides vitamin E. The betacarotene content is destroyed when the oil is refined, which it is for the majority of use but some unrefined palm oil is available. Unrefined palm oil can be

Above: Oil is pressed from coconut flesh (copra) which is dried in the sun.

Above: Coconut oil is predominantly used in South Asian cooking.

found in some African stores and blended with other oils, for example with rapeseed (canola) oil. The palm oil may be referred to as 'red palm oil' or 'red palm fruit oil'. *Palm kernel oil* is extracted from the kernel of the nut and it is quite different in composition from palm oil, with a high percentage of saturated fat (about 80 per cent). Unlike the oil from the fruit, the kernel oil is pale in colour and does not contain betacarotene.

Palm oil and palm kernel oil are both widely used in margarine and commercial food production, including fats, vegetable oils and shortenings, peanut butter, baked goods, ice creams and snacks.

USE
- As a cooking medium for frying, roasting or baking (check the ingredients if using a blended oil).
- In marinades, dressings or sauces.

Coconut or copra oil

Copra is the term for dried coconut flesh, which contains 65 to 70 per cent oil. Coconut oil is extracted from the dried flesh and widely used in commercially prepared food products, such as baked goods and margarine. It is also used as a cooking oil, especially in some regions of India.

Coconut oil contains high levels of saturated fatty acids. The oil is also used in the cosmetics industry and in soap production. It can also be used as a fuel for diesel engines.

USE
- As a cooking medium, especially when frying.
- To add an authentic flavour to South Asian dishes such as sauces or curries.
- In natural skincare remedies.
- As a carrier oil for massage.

Above: The high betacarotene content in palm oil gives it a distinct red colour.

Above: Soya beans are native to East Asia. They are harvested and used in tofu and soy sauce as well as oil.

Above: Soya beans, and their oil, are a good source of protein and often used as a dairy substitute.

They contain about 50 per cent fat that is mainly polyunsaturated. The oil has the great advantage of a long shelf life as it does not turn rancid easily.

Plain sesame oil is light in colour and mildly but very distinctly flavoured. Toasted sesame oil is the product of the toasted seeds and this is far darker in colour and much stronger in flavour.

Sesame oil is added to margarine and used in cooking, usually in a relatively modest proportion to bring flavour, while a plainer oil that does not burn as easily is used for the purpose of frying. Both plain and toasted sesame oils are often used in Asian dishes.

Soya oil

The soya beans that are used to make soya oil are better known in the domestic sense as whole beans, or for the many products that use the whole bean, such as tofu and soy sauce. Although soya beans contain a relatively modest proportion of oil (14 to 24 per cent) it is highly unsaturated and it is one of the most important vegetable oils. Soya oil is widely used in blended vegetable oils, margarines and in food products.

USE
- As a cooking medium, for frying, roasting and baking.
- For marinating.
- As a base for salad dressings or in sauces.

Sesame oil

An ancient oil-producing crop, the cultivation of sesame originated in Africa, from where it spread to India and throughout Asia, on to America. Sesame seeds are the fruit of an annual plant and they are just as important whole as they are for oil production.

USE
- In frying or stir-frying to prevent the oil from overcooking at high temperature and becoming bitter. Add a little to cooking part-way through.
- In marinades and sauces.
- In small quantities in salad dressings and cold sauces or dips.
- As a base oil for massage.

CASTOR OIL

Extracted from the seeds of the castor oil plant, castor oil is not an 'edible' oil in the culinary sense but an old-fashioned purgative or laxative.

Above: Plain sesame oil is light in colour but has a strong sesame flavour.

Above: Oil made from toasted seeds is darker in colour than plain sesame oil.

Sunflower oil

Native Americans have used sunflowers for thousands of years in their breads and as a source of oil. The seeds were introduced to Europe by early explorers and on to Russia in the 19th century. The Ukraine takes the credit for invention of the first sunflower mill specifically for oil extraction. Russia and France are important producers of sunflower oil outside the United States.

Sunflower seeds vary in their composition but the fat content is between about 25 to 50 per cent, with a high proportion of polyunsaturated fatty acids. Before olive oil increased in popularity with the increased interest in monounsaturated fat, sunflower oil was promoted as the healthy alternative to saturated fats.

Sunflower oil is widely used in spreads, shortenings and margarines as well as in mixed vegetable oils.

USE
- As a cooking medium for frying, roasting, baking and in baking mixtures.
- In salad dressings and sauces.

Above: Fields of yellow rape can be seen throughout Europe, as well as in Canada, the United States, China and India.

Rapeseed (canola) oil

The rape plant is also known as cole, coleseed or colza as well as canola. The name 'canola' originally derived from the phrase 'Canadian oil, low acid'.

The two main varieties of rape that are widely cultivated include oilseed rape or swede rape (*Brassica napus*)

Above: The mild oil produced from rape is yellow in colour, and is a good source of essential fatty acids.

and turnip rape, toria or sarson (*Brassica rapa*). While there is evidence of rape having been grown across China and India some 2000 years ago, it is relatively new on the commercial oil scene. The oil was originally used in Asia and Europe in lamps. Rape seeds contain about 40 per cent oil, which is highly unsaturated with a large proportion of monounsaturated fats. The oil is rich in both omega-6 and omega-3 fatty acids.

The bright yellow rape crop is now grown across Canada, China, India and Europe. The resulting oil is yellow in colour, mild and light but with a distinct flavour. Its aroma is mild and almost floral, with some similarity to a sweet corn kernel aroma. The oil is used as a cooking oil and in margarine production. It is used widely in Scandinavia.

USE
- As a cooking medium, for frying, roasting or baking.
- In dressings and marinades.

Above: Sunflower oil has a light flavour, and is used most commonly as a frying oil.

Above: Sunflower seeds are pressed for oil, which has a high vitamin E content.

Rice bran oil

A pale yellow oil with a light texture and bland flavour, rice bran oil is the oil extracted from the germ and husk of rice. It is highly unsaturated (about 75 per cent) with a high proportion of monounsaturates and a good vitamin E content.

The filtered cold pressed oil has a high smoking point of 490°F/254°C and therefore it is recommended for frying and as a cooking medium. It has been used in vegetable ghee, which is sold as an alternative to dairy ghee.

The light flavour of rice bran oil makes it suitable for salad dressings and sauces, especially when highly flavoured nut oils are added or if the flavour accent of other ingredients is required. It is a popular cooking ingredient in Japan and China.

USE

- For high-temperature cooking methods such as stir-frying and deep-frying.
- In dressings and sauces where a mild flavour is preferred.

Above: Corn or maize oil retains a distinct corn flavour when cold pressed.

Above: Safflower oil is similar to sunflower oil in appearance and nutritional content.

Safflower oil

A relative newcomer to modern global cooking oils, safflowers were originally grown for their brightly coloured petals rather than their seeds. The petals were sold as 'false saffron', as a cheaper alternative to the real thing, and also made into dye. The safflower plant resembles a thistle or small globe artichoke with bright yellow, orange or red coloured petals. Safflower seeds produce an oil with a high level of polyunsaturated fats and a light flavour.

USE

- In gentle cooking and in cold dishes, dressings and sauces.
- As a base oil for massage.

Corn or maize oil

As well as oil from the germ, which contains about 25 to 50 per cent fat that is largely polyunsaturated, corn provides starch. Cold pressed, unrefined corn oil has a distinct flavour of corn, while the refined oil is far lighter in flavour and colour. Both types are used as a general cooking

Above: Safflowers are grown commercially in more than 60 countries worldwide.

medium in the same way as sunflower or vegetable oil as well as for salad dressings, salsas and dips.

USE

- In marinades, batters or baking for distinct flavour (cold pressed corn oil is best for this).
- To contribute a distinct corn flavour to fried foods, such as chicken or corn fritters.
- For all general cooking when a strong flavour is not required (use refined corn oil).
- For salad dressings, salsas, dips and other cold dishes (both types can be used for this).

Wheatgerm oil

Cold pressed wheatgerm oil is valued for its high vitamin E content. It is largely polyunsaturated with a light mild flavour.

The oil is expensive and generally promoted as a supplement rather than a culinary ingredient, with manufacturer's recommendations provided for daily dosage. Its high vitamin E content also makes it useful for beauty products, such as hand and face creams and face masks or moisturizing scrubs.

USE
- In cold dishes, such as salad dressings or sauces.
- In natural skincare remedies.
- As a base oil for massage.

Cottonseed oil

With a content of about 50 per cent polyunsaturated fatty acids, cottonseed oil is used as a general cooking oil and in the production of margarine. It is often used in manufacturing potato crisps (US potato chips) and other snack foods. Early in the 20th century, several grades of cottonseed oil were produced, some with a 'pleasantly nutty taste' according to an early guide to groceries. Cottonseed oil was widely used to adulterate olive oil.

USE
- As a cooking medium, for frying, roasting or baking.

Above: Wheatgerm oil is used mainly as a health supplement and in cosmetics.

Above: Oil has been extracted from the seeds of the flax plant for centuries.

Flax or linseed oil

Linseed oil is extracted from the seeds of the flax plant. It has a long history of cultivation and culinary use in Russia and Eastern European countries, especially Silesia, a region of Poland, and the Czech Republic and Slovak Republic. Linseeds are small, shiny, brown seeds that contribute an excellent texture to roasted seed mixtures, breads and similar baked goods. The oil is not widely used for cooking (better known in the paint industry and for wood preservation) but it is now popular for the polyunsaturated fats it contains, especially omega-3 and omega-6.

The cold pressed oil has a distinctive aroma, golden colour and bitter flavour. It becomes rancid relatively quickly and manufacturers recommend that opened bottles should be stored in the refrigerator. It is not suitable as a cooking medium but can be used as a dressing on hot or cold foods. Traditionally, it is used to dress potatoes and other vegetables.

Healthfood brands, including those sold through supermarkets, suggest taking the oil as a supplement rather than using

Above: Linseed oil is not used in cooking, and is better as a dressing ingredient.

it in cooking. Its distinctive bitter flavour makes this oil a difficult ingredient that needs to be carefully balanced and it is something of an acquired taste.

Russia, India and South America were the traditional producers of linseed oil a century ago. Baltic and Black Sea oils were obtained from Russia, East India oil from India and River Plate oil from South America. The Baltic oil was the better quality of the Russian and Indian oils as it was less likely to be adulterated by foreign seeds of other plant varieties. The oils were imported into Britain for use in the painting and decorating trades.

USE
- The oil may be taken in small doses as a health supplement.
- As a dressing – mix with apple juice and honey, adding a little lemon for a refreshing sharpness that is different from the bitterness of the oil.
- To drizzle over mild yogurt and soft cheeses; add honey or syrup for a little sweetness to make a creamy dressing for salads or vegetables.

Avocado oil

The flesh of an avocado contains about
30 per cent oil, with a good percentage
of monounsaturated fats. Avocado oil
has a light yet distinct avocado flavour
and the unmistakable richness of the
avocado. It makes an excellent dressing
for salads that include avocado and it
can be used in guacamole or other
avocado dips. Refined avocado oil is
also produced and recommended for
use as a cooking medium.

   Avocado oil can be used for home-
made beauty products, in moisturizing
face masks, hand and foot treatments.

USE

- In cold dressings, especially with light
  vinegars, lemon or lime juice.
- To drizzle over salami, cold meats,
  smoked fish or cheese.
- As a dressing for fruit, such as papaya, in
  savoury salads and dishes.
- For moistening grilled (broiled) fish.
- For enriching avocado dips or other dips
  and sauces.
- In mayonnaise for a richer flavour.

*Above: Grape seed oil varies in flavour
and colour, from strongly flavoured green
to much lighter refined varieties.*

*Above: Avocado oil can be added to dips
such as guacamole for a rich flavour.*

Grape seed oil

While cold pressed grape seed oil is
green with a pronounced flavour, there
are also very light and flavourless, refined
grape seed oils. Refined grape seed oil
can be used as a cooking medium;
however, it is an expensive choice. Cold
pressed oil can also be used for cooking
but it is better suited to cold preparation.

   A good source of vitamin E and alpha-
lineolenic acid, grape seed oil is also used
commercially in cosmetics and can be
useful for making moisturizing treatments.

USE

- To moisten fish and poultry before
  baking in the oven.
- As a medium for frying.
- In marinades for fish, poultry, meat
  or vegetables.
- In salad dressings, dips and salsas.

Plum seed oil

A French product, this is extracted
from the kernels of plums grown for
drying to produce prunes d'Agen.
The oil is highly unsaturated with
about 70 per cent monounsaturated

*Above: Pumpkin seed oil retains the
mild nutty flavour of the seeds.*

and 20 per cent polyunsaturated
fats. The key characteristic of the oil
is its fabulous almond-like flavour.
The expensive oil is used as a dressing
or flavouring ingredient.

USE

- In dressings, dips and sauces, savoury
  or sweet.
- For drizzling over fruit or desserts,
  combining with syrups or stirring
  into creams.

Pumpkin seed oil

The cultivation of pumpkins originates
from South America and Mexico, with
certain species being cultivated for their
seeds. The seeds contain about 45 per
cent fat, largely polyunsaturated. The oil
is dark green and viscose with a full
flavour that is mild and nutty. The oil is
expensive and useful for cold preparation.

USE

- As a dipping oil, with bread.
- In salad dressings, sauces and dips.
- To drizzle over cooked foods or dishes,
  or into soups.

Argan oil

The argan tree (*Argania spinosa*) is an evergreen that is native to Morocco. The oil is extracted from the seeds of its fruit. The cold pressed oil is rich in vitamin E and alpha-linoleic acid. It has a distinct flavour and nutty, toasted aroma, with a hint of sharpness but not bitterness.

Argan oil is expensive and useful for cold cooking or dressing hot or warm food rather than as a cooking medium.

USE
- As a dipping oil for breads.
- In salad dressings or to drizzle over cooked meats, vegetables, cheese or cooked dishes, such as tagines.

Hemp seed oil

A member of the cannabis family, hemp is the name for a plant from which yarns are obtained. Cannabis is illegal in most countries, and seeds used for oil have to be free from the substance associated with cannabis used as a drug. The golden-coloured oil available from supermarket ranges is refined and lighter than the deep

Above: Oil is extracted from the seed of the hemp plant, commonly used for fabrics.

green cold pressed oil with a strong flavour. The golden oil has a distinctly green or grassy flavour, with a slight bitterness but less so than linseed oil.

Hemp seed oil can be used in warm or cold dishes but not as a cooking medium. The oil is a good source of omega-3 and omega-6 fatty acids.

Above: Poppy seeds are edible and have been used in cooking for many years.

USE
- As a supplement. The oil may be taken in small doses following the manufacturer's instructions.
- Combined with sweet and sharp ingredients to make dressings.
- Drizzled into portions of vegetable soups or dips that will benefit from the 'freshness' of its green flavour.
- Complemented with lime or lemon rind and juice.

Poppy seed oil

The seeds of the poppy flower have been used in cooking for thousands of years. Poppy seed oil has a subtle flavour and is used in dressings and as a condiment for bread rather than as a cooking oil.

The oil is rich in omega-6 fatty acids, and is used in the production of skincare products and soaps, as well as in the manufacture of paints and varnishes.

Above: Roasted argan seeds are ground into oil by hand. The oil is expensive, and has a distinct nutty flavour.

Above: The evergreen argan tree is native to Morocco. Each fruit contains 1–3 of the small oil-rich seeds.

USE
- As a condiment or dip for bread.
- In salad dressings.

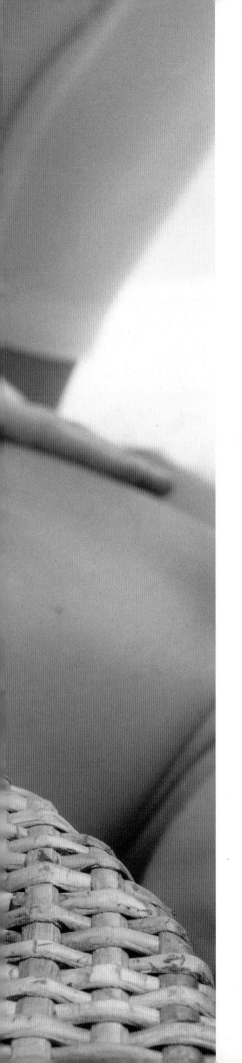

OILS FOR HEALTH AND HEALING

Oils play numerous roles in promoting good health, featuring in the ancient practice of massage therapy as well as playing an essential part in a balanced diet. Adding just a few drops of a favourite essential oil for massage will transform a simple vegetable carrier oil, giving it relaxing, soothing or healing powers. Oils are vital for our health and wellbeing, and can be used to treat various ailments such as head lice, insomnia, colds, headaches, spots, burns, bites, bruises or stings.

Left: Massage oils consist of a small amount of a chosen essential oil which is blended with a vegetable carrier oil.

VEGETABLE OILS AND MASSAGE

One of the main contemporary uses of oil as an aid to health and wellbeing is as a medium in massage. Massage aids relaxation, helps tired or strained muscles and can ease health problems.

Massage is one of the oldest therapies, and oils have been used in massage for thousands of years. Massage reduces tension and stress, can ease tired muscles and aching limbs, energize your whole being and even alleviate certain complaints.

Carrier oil basics

In massage, small amounts of different essential oils are dissolved in a vegetable carrier oil to make a blend that makes it easier to move the hands continuously on the skin without dragging or slipping. Choosing an appropriate carrier oil will heighten the dynamic nature of a massage and can have specific benefits, such as helping to guard against heart disease or inflammatory diseases such as arthritis. It can also help to boost the immune system. When used in massage, vegetable carrier oils can be absorbed into the blood stream through the skin's pores.

Vegetable oils are made up of essential fatty acids and contain the fat-soluble vitamins A, D, and E. Some oils also contain large amounts of gamma linoleic acid (GLA), useful for the treatment of PMS. The fatty acid compounds help to reduce blood cholesterol levels and strengthen cell membranes, slowing down the formation of fine lines and wrinkles and helping the body to resist attack from free radicals.

Heat-treated oils lose their nutritional value, so always use a cold pressed, unrefined vegetable oil

Above: Almond oil (front) is gentle and is suitable for most skin types, including very dry or dehydrated skin. Grape seed oil (left) has almost no smell, so is ideal for blending with essential oils. Olive oil (back right) is easy to get hold of, but it does have a strong smell that can be difficult to disguise.

as a carrier for essential oils. Likewise, use a certified organic vegetable oil, as this guarantees that no chemical fertilizers, pesticides, or fungicides have been used in its production. The darker the colour and stronger the odour, the less refined the oil, so it will be richer in health-giving properties.

Vegetable carrier oils

The following oils can be used alone, or as a carrier for essential oils. Once opened, store in the refrigerator.

Almond oil A good source of vitamin D. It is suitable for all skin types, but is especially good for dry or irritated skin.

Sweet almond oil is one of the most versatile carrier oils. It is easily absorbed and is a warming, light oil. It can help to relieve muscular pain and stiffness.

Avocado oil Easily absorbed into the skin, it is excellent for dry or mature skin. It can help to relieve the dryness and itching of psoriasis and eczema. It blends well with other oils, and its fruity smell may influence which essential oils you choose.

Coconut oil Light coconut oil is used extensively in traditional Indian head massage. It is easy to use and blends well with essential oils.

Grape seed oil A non-greasy oil that suits all skin types. This oil is not usable as a cold pressed oil but is widely available in a refined state and is best enriched with almond oil.

Hazelnut oil Its astringent qualities make it a useful carrier oil for oily and combination skins.

Olive oil Too sticky for massage, but excellent in a blend for mature or dry skin. Use the best quality virgin, extra virgin or cold-pressed oils as these contain high levels of unsaturated fatty acids that are nourishing for dry skin and hair.

Groundnut (peanut) oil This is best when unrefined, but rarely available. Its refined form makes a good base oil for massage, but is best enriched with a more nutritious oil if you require more than just a slippage medium.

Safflower oil This is light and penetrates the skin well. Cheap and readily available in an unrefined state, it is a useful base oil.

Sesame oil When made from untoasted seeds, sesame oil is very good for treating skin conditions. It has sunscreening properties and is used in many suncare products. Use commercial preparations with a stated SPF number. In Ayurveda, sesame oil is very popular for massaging the head and body. It helps to strengthen, condition and moisturize the skin and hair. It is a balancing oil and can help to reduce pain and swelling.

Sunflower oil A light oil rich in vitamins and minerals. It can be enriched by the addition of more exotic oils.

Walnut oil This contains small amounts of essential fatty acids and has a pleasant, nutty aroma.

Wheatgerm oil Rich in vitamin E and useful for dry and mature skin. It is well known for its ability to heal scar tissue, reduce stretch marks, and soothe burns. It is too sticky as a massage oil, so add small amounts of it to a lighter oil. It should not be used on people with wheat intolerance.

BLENDING OILS FOR MASSAGE

Experiment with different types of carrier oil to achieve the ideal blend for your massage style. Try adding a teaspoonful of another carrier oil as well as the essential oils for a highly personal mixture. It is worth remembering that even the weather affects the state of our skin, and in the winter central heating and cold temperatures will cause it to dry out. These variations can be accommodated by changing the exotic carrier oils used to enrich each blend.

Rub a little of the blend between the palms of your hands to warm it, then test the fragrance before beginning the massage. It may require slight adjustment before you are happy with the result.

Before you begin blending the oils, wash and dry your hands and make sure that you have all the bowls and bottles you need, and that all your utensils are clean and dry. Have your essential oils at the ready, but leave the lids on the bottles until they are required.

Measure out approximately 10ml/2 tsp of your chosen carrier oil and gently pour it into your blending bowl.

Bearing in mind the correct ratio of essential oil to carrier oil (generally 10ml/2 tsp base oil to 3–5 drops of essential oil, but check labels for guidance) add the first essential oil a drop at a time. Add remaining oils a drop at a time and mix gently with a clean, dry cocktail stick or toothpick, to blend.

Above: Generally, add 3–5 drops of essential oil to 10ml/2 tsp carrier oil. Check labels for individual instructions.

Above: Warm a small amount of your blended oil in the palms of your hands to test the fragrance.

ESSENTIAL OILS

An essential oil is the essence of a plant, the plant's life force distilled for use. The oils are extracted from many different parts of a plant – leaves, flowers, fruits or other material.

Essential oils should not be applied undiluted to the skin, but should be mixed first, in the right proportions, in a vegetable carrier oil. Massage is just one use for essential oils, but when there is not time for a massage, adding a few drops of oil to a bath or foot soak is also beneficial. Both soaking and inhaling make use of the different health-giving properties of the oils.

Useful essential oils for health

Benzoin The tree gum is available in dissolved form. It is the key ingredient in Friar's Balsam. Known for clearing the head and useful for healing, for example to treat dry rough skin or chilblains.

Bergamot This is obtained from the rind of a citrus fruit. It is a bright and uplifting oil, which is helpful for overcoming anxiety and depression. It is also used to assist in the treatment of urinary tract infections such as cystitis.

Eucalyptus This is good for muscular pain and is effective against coughs and colds, both as a preventative and as a remedy.

Frankincense Known for its sedative and anti-inflammatory qualities, this calming oil also has antiseptic qualities and it is helpful for easing coughs and bronchitis. Frankincense is thought to help slow and deepen breathing, which makes it helpful for overcoming anxiety.

Geranium The aroma of geranium oil makes it valuable in beauty potions and lotions. It is antiseptic with astringent characteristics and known as a balancing oil that can be helpful for skins that may be too oily or dry. It has antidepressant qualities and is said to be calming.

Juniper Known for its antiseptic, astringent, cleansing and diuretic qualities, juniper is thought of as a detoxifying oil for the body and useful for settling and sorting racing minds. Mentally, it can act in a restorative sense. It is also thought to help reduce cellulite.

Lavender One of the most popular oils, lavender is calming, soothing and balancing. It is also antiseptic and healing. Lavender is versatile and one of the most useful oils for helping with all types of healing, including improving bad skin and soothing minor burns. Lavender is also helpful for inducing sleep or overcoming insomnia. A lavender bath, massage or just a little massaged into the wrists before bed helps with sleep. It is also a good oil to use for massaging tired muscles and for a soothing, de-stressing shoulder massage or head massage.

Lemon A lively oil that is thought to help stimulate the immune system, lemon is also anti-bacterial and good for cleansing cuts. It is also astringent and antiseptic. It is an uplifting and stimulating oil, helpful for overcoming depression.

Marjoram A warming oil that can be used to clear the head and ease coughs associated with a cold. Marjoram is a sedative and sleep-inducing, and it can numb the senses. It is also thought to aid digestion and ease indigestion. It is said to be helpful for easing menstrual cramps.

Myrrh Anti-inflammatory and expectorant, myrrh will help to ease bronchitis, catarrh, coughs and colds. Also good for digestive problems, infections of the mouth and throat, and skin conditions.

Above: Essential oils should be mixed with a vegetable carrier oil before they are applied to the skin. Always check the label for the recommended quantity to use, as it can vary.

Neroli An orange-blossom oil, this is another oil that is helpful for calming and reducing anxiety. It has anti-depressant and soothing qualities, and is helpful for promoting relaxation and sleep. Neroli is useful in skin lotions and it is thought to stimulate skin regeneration and help to reduce the effects of ageing.

Palma rosa This is good for the skin and is also used to relieve stiff and sore muscles, while calming the mind and uplifting and invigorating the spirits. Often used in soaps, perfumes and cosmetics.

ESSENTIAL OIL WARNINGS

- Always use essential oils diluted.

- Never take essential oils internally unless professionally prescribed.

- Do not use the same essential oils for more than one or two weeks at any one time.

- For problem or sensitive skin, dilute the oils further. If any irritation occurs, stop using them.

- Some oils, such as bergamot, make the skin more sensitive to the sun, so use with caution.

- Essential oils should be used only according to medical and professional aromatherapy advice during pregnancy as some should be avoided.

- Similarly, because the oils can be powerful and in some cases the effects can be cumulative, those suffering from medical conditions or who suspect they have a problem should seek medical advice.

- Essential oils can be helpful and can complement some other treatment but using the appropriate oils and techniques is vital.

- If you are unsure about the suitability of an oil, always seek the advice of a qualified aromatherapist.

Patchouli An oil with a distinct aroma, patchouli is known as antiseptic and anti-inflammatory. It can be used for skincare and for haircare, to promote good scalp health and help overcome dandruff. Patchouli is also thought of as an aphrodisiac and anti-depressant.

Peppermint Uplifting and stimulating, peppermint oil is thought to help overcome fatigue and ease headaches. It has antiseptic and antispasmodic properties, and is helpful for overcoming indigestion and upset stomachs.

Pine Antiseptic and decongestant, pine is known as one of the head-clearing oils that are excellent for inhaling or adding to baths to relieve a bad cold. Along with eucalyptus, it is useful for relieving sinus congestion and it is also thought to help sooth coughs. Pine is a stimulating oil, and is helpful for promoting circulation and for treating aching muscles.

Rose One of the favourite essential oils, valued for skincare and beauty products. Rose oil is anti-depressant and calming, soothing and helpful for overcoming insomnia. It is widely used in aromatherapy to treat a wide variety of conditions, from menstrual to sexual problems, depression and nervousness. Rose oil is thought of as a general tonic among essential oils.

Rosemary Rosemary oil is a powerful stimulant. It is known for astringent and head-clearing qualities, which include decongestant properties as well as an ability to promote clear thinking. It is also useful for relieving muscular pain. Rosemary oil is also useful for haircare, in rinses and conditioners. Being a strong stimulant, rosemary oil should not be used by anyone with epilepsy.

Rosewood A calming and soothing oil that has antiseptic properties, rosewood is useful for overcoming stress and

Above: There are many essential oils which are beneficial to the health.

depression. It is anti-bacterial and antiseptic and a mild oil for beauty products and skincare.

Sandalwood A soothing, anti-depressant and aphrodisiac oil, sandalwood has antiseptic properties and has long been used to help overcome urinary tract infections. One of its main uses is as a balancing oil for skincare, overcoming both dryness and excess oiliness.

Tea tree This oil has strong antiseptic properties with a matching aroma. It has excellent antimicrobial and antifungal action. It is a powerful stimulant to the immune system.

Thyme An antiseptic oil that stimulates digestion and helps to clear congestion. Thyme is thought of as a balancing oil, being calming or stimulating, helping to promote sleep, relieve fatigue and overcome depression.

Ylang-ylang An oil with a sweet, heavy aroma, ylang-ylang is anti-depressant, calming and sleep inducing. It is said to be useful for reducing blood pressure, promoting relaxation and easing stress. It is also said to have aphrodisiac qualities.

NATURAL REMEDIES WITH OILS

Vegetable oils can be used to treat a wide variety of minor ailments whether used on their own or mixed with essential oils, herbs or other ingredients.

Aromatherapy compress

Applying an aromatherapy compress will help to ease bruising, pain or arthritic joints. Use a warm compress for general pain, aching or arthritic joints, and a cold compress if the area is inflamed, swollen or hot.

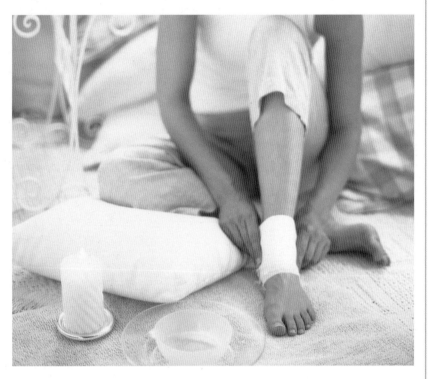

INGREDIENTS

10ml/2 tsp grape seed oil

4 drops geranium essential oil

3 drops bergamot essential oil

3 drops clary sage essential oil

1 Put the grape seed oil in a small bowl, then add the essential oils and blend.

2 Add the blended oils to a bowl of hot or very cold water and mix.

3 Soak a small towel or facecloth in the water, wring it out and hold on the affected area. Replace the cloth often so that the temperature remains constant.

Health tip

To make an aromatic ice-pack, freeze the same essential oil and water mix in an ice-cube tray. Never apply ice directly to the skin. Wrap the aromatic ice cubes in a cloth and apply to the affected area.

Oil pulling

This is an alternative therapy which has its origins in ancient Ayurvedic writings.

A small amount of oil is held in the mouth every morning for up to 20 minutes. Sesame or sunflower are the recommended oils to use. This must be done on an empty stomach, and the oil must not be swallowed.

The oil is swished around the mouth, pulled through the teeth (hence the name of the therapy) and then spat out after a maximum of 20 minutes. The mouth is then rinsed out thoroughly with 2 or 3 glasses of cold water.

The idea behind the therapy is that toxins are pulled out of the body into the oil, then removed from the body altogether when the practitioner spits out the oil.

It has been claimed that oil pulling can help with many illnesses and complaints, from headaches and migraines to eczema and ulcers, although there is currently no scientific evidence to support this.

Energy boosting massage cream

Use this cream for a soothing and revitalizing massage session.

INGREDIENTS

20ml/4 tsp almond oil

40ml/8 tsp avocado oil

20ml/4 tsp rosewater

5ml/1 tsp lecithin granules

10g/^{1}/4fl oz beeswax

8 drops each pettigrain and peppermint
  essential oils

1 Put the almond oil, avocado oil and beeswax into a ceramic or stainless steel jug (pitcher). Stand in a pan that is half-filled with water.

2 Heat on a low temperature, stirring occasionally until the wax melts. Remove the jug from the water.

3 Add the lecithin and beat the mixture vigorously, then stir in the rosewater.

4 Allow the mixture to cool slightly, then mix in the pettigrain and peppermint essential oils and transfer into a clean screw-top jar. Store in a cool dark place. This will last for about 12 treatments.

Rheumatism liniment

A liniment is a liquid preparation, often made by mixing a herb oil with a tincture. For rheumatic pains, aching joints and tired muscles, rub this liniment gently into the affected areas. It should be applied to the skin at body temperature. Do not apply to broken skin.

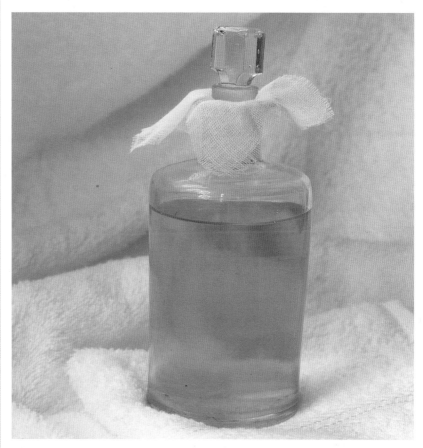

INGREDIENTS

6 garlic cloves, crushed

300ml/^{1}/2 pint/1^1/4 cups olive oil

For the juniper tincture

15g/^{1}/2oz dried juniper berries

250ml/8fl oz/1 cup vodka

50ml/^{1}/4 cup water

1 First make the juniper tincture. Add the dried juniper berries to a glass jar. Pour in the vodka and water. Put the lid on and leave in a cool, dark place for 7–10 days (no longer), shaking occasionally.

2 Stain through a sieve (strainer) lined with kitchen paper before pouring into a sterilized glass bottle. Seal with a cork. The tincture will keep for up to 2 years.

3 Put the crushed garlic cloves in a bowl and pour over the olive oil.

4 Cover the bowl with a piece of foil and stand it over a pan of simmering water. Heat gently for 1 hour. Check the water level regularly and top up as necessary.

5 Strain the oil, allow to cool, then stir in the tincture of juniper and pour into a stoppered bottle. This will keep for several months if stored in a cool dark place.

Variation

Juniper tincture can be taken internally but contains alcohol so should not be given to children. Take no more than 5ml/ 1 tsp, 3–4 times a day, diluted in water or fruit juice if preferred.

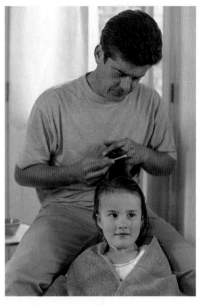

Head lice treatment

A common problem among school-age children, head lice (nits) can be difficult to eradicate. Using essential oils offers a natural solution.

INGREDIENTS

30ml/2 tbsp coconut or almond oil

5 drops lavender essential oil

5 drops geranium essential oil

5 drops eucalyptus essential oil

1 Combine all the ingredients and apply the mixture all over the head and hair, massaging it in well.

2 Cover the head and leave the oils in for a minimum of 4 hours, although overnight is better.

3 To remove the oil, massage shampoo into the hair before applying water, then wash and rinse as usual. Comb through the hair with a lice comb.

4 Repeat the whole process after 24 hours and again after 8 days. This will give you the opportunity to treat any lice that have hatched since the first treatment. The treatment should be stored in a dark glass jar for up to 12 months.

Insomnia massage spray

This massage spray contains chamomile and lavender essential oils, which are both prized for their relaxing and sedative properties. Giving yourself a foot massage at bedtime will help you to relax and drift off to sleep.

INGREDIENTS

25ml/5 tsp grape seed oil

25ml/5 tsp almond oil

20ml/4 tsp jojoba oil

10ml/2 tsp rosewater

10ml/2 tsp glycerine

20 drops each lavender and chamomile
    essential oils

1 Mix the grape seed oil, almond oil, jojoba oil, rosewater and glycerine together in a small bowl.

2 Stir in the essential oils, mixing well. Transfer to a clean spray bottle.

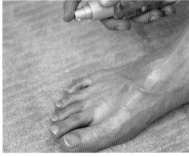

3 Sit in a comfortable chair or lie down in bed. Spray a little of the mixture on to each foot, or on to a large, clean tissue and wipe both feet with the tissue.

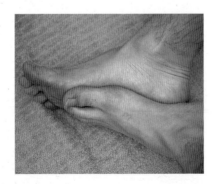

4 Use your feet to massage each other.

Hair repair

Olive oil has been used as a hair and scalp conditioner since ancient times. Use this hair repair as an intensive, deep-conditioning treatment once a month for hair that is thinning.

INGREDIENTS

30ml/2 tbsp olive oil

10ml/2 tsp wheatgerm oil

8 drops rosemary essential oil

6 drops patchouli oil

1 drop lavender essential oil

1 Mix olive oil and wheatgerm oil together in a small glass bowl.

2 Add the rosemary, patchouli and lavender essential oils.

3 Massage the oil mixture into the hair and leave overnight. (Protect your pillow with a towel.) Rinse off thoroughly the next day.

Health tip

Warm a little olive oil in the palm of your hand and massage into the scalp once a week to treat dandruff.

OLD-FASHIONED OIL REMEDIES

Olive oil was traditionally sold in small corked bottles in chemists' shops and used in small amounts for many treatments that would not be recommended today, for example, a little warm olive oil was trickled into the ear to help relieve earache. Some of the following are included out of fascination rather than recommendation, as today we have alternative remedies.

BOWEL PROBLEMS One of the traditional reasons for taking spoonfuls of olive oil as a supplement was to overcome constipation. In more extreme circumstances castor oil was taken. A dose of castor oil was also recommended for anyone suffering from diarrhoea, the idea being to expel as much as possible of the cause of the problem before taking a remedy to prevent the problem. One cure for diarrhoea, to be taken after the oil and said to 'act like magic' was a mixture of 5ml/1 tsp salt and 15ml/1 tbsp vinegar.

SCALDS A mixture of equal quantities of lime water and linseed oil were used to treat scalds – a piece of linen cloth was soaked in the mixture and applied to the scalded area.

SORE THROAT AND LOST VOICE When a sore throat leads to a lost voice, people used to gargle with warm olive oil. The idea of gargling with pure olive oil seems a little extreme, but using a mixture of half oil and half hot water (from a boiling kettle) would seem soothing. Follow by slowly sucking a teaspoon of honey, which is excellent for the throat as it is a natural antiseptic.

Lavender and eucalyptus vapour rub for colds

A blocked nose is a misery when suffering from a cold and prevents a sound night's sleep. This decongestant rub has a warming and soothing action and should be rubbed gently on to the throat, chest and back at bedtime, so that the vapours can be inhaled throughout the night. It can also be inhaled in boiling water. Known particularly for its head-clearing properties, eucalyptus oil is common in decongestants and inhalers.

INGREDIENTS

50g/2oz petroleum jelly

15ml/1 tbsp dried lavender

6 drops eucalyptus essential oil

4 drops camphor essential oil

1 Melt the petroleum jelly in a bowl over a pan of simmering water. Stir in the lavender and heat for about 30 minutes.

2 Strain the through muslin (cheesecloth), leave to cool slightly, then add the eucalyptus and camphor essential oils.

3 Pour into a clean jar and leave until the rub is set. Store in a cool, dark place and use within 1 month.

Headache remedy

Lavender essential oil can help to soothe headaches.

Add a few drops of lavender oil to a clean tissue and sniff throughout the day to relieve headaches.

Essential oil inhalant

Inhaling steam scented with aromatic essential oils is an excellent way to relieve the congestion of a cold or blocked sinuses. Try the combination of oils below, or use other decongestant essential oils such as cinnamon, eucalyptus, lavender, lemon, marjoram, peppermint or pine.

INGREDIENTS

600ml/1 pint/2^1/2 cups boiling water

5 drops eucalyptus essential oil

2 drops camphor essential oil

1 drop citronella essential oil

1 Pour the boiling water into a large bowl.

2 Add the eucalyptus, camphor and citronella essential oils to the water.

3 Sitting at a table with the bowl in front of you, lean forwards over the bowl, covering your head with a towel to keep the steam in.

4 Inhale the scented steam for about 5–10 minutes, but stop if your face becomes overheated or you feel uncomfortably warm.

Burns, bites, bruises or stings

This simple oil-based mixture can be used to soothe minor burns, bites, bruises or skin blemishes.

Pour 25ml/1^1/2 tbsp sunflower oil or almond oil in a small glass jar. Add 15ml/ 1 tbsp lavender essential oil and mix together thoroughly.

BUYING ESSENTIAL OILS

Always buy essential oils from a reputable supplier to be sure of obtaining the pure and concentrated oils. Good quality essential oils are expensive, so be wary of any exceptionally cheap oils. They should be purchased in small quantities and stored in small dark-glass bottles with airtight tops in a cool, dark place. A dropper and small funnel are useful for measuring and mixing.

Essential oil burner

Plant essential oils have a powerful effect – breathing in their vapours can be relaxing, restorative or uplifting.

Put a few drops of oil on a handkerchief and keep it on your pillow overnight. For a more controlled and concentrated method, an essential oil burner is the answer.

Spot treatment

To combat troublesome spots, use a mixture of lavender oil and olive oil.

Add 1–2 drops of lavender essential oil to a little olive oil and apply to the problem area with a small piece of cotton wool (cotton balls).

NATURAL BEAUTY WITH OILS

There are very good reasons for using vegetable oils and essential oils as part of a regular routine without giving up a favourite face freshener or body lotion. The natural moisturizing and conditioning qualities of oil have been recognized for thousands of years. Occasional oil-based beauty products such as hair conditioners, face packs, foot lotions and hand conditioners can all be made at home cheaply and easily for use as a special treat to boost everyday beauty regimes.

Left: Vegetable oils are very good for the skin and hair — they are rich in vitamin E and are natural moisturizers.

OIL AND BEAUTY

A variety of oils can be used to prepare home-made natural beauty remedies. Use them in relaxing bath oils, moisturizing body creams and face masks.

Oils have long been associated with beauty and skincare. Egyptian men and women oiled their skin and hair throughout the day with almond oil scented with frankincense and myrrh. The ancient Greeks and Romans certainly knew that olive oil was good for the skin, and used it after baths, before meals, before and after exercise and before and after journeys. The Greek philosopher Democritus had a simple recipe for health: honey on the inside and oil on the outside.

Oils have been used for many centuries to ease tired muscles, soften rough skin and soothe abrasions. They are also a traditional conditioning treatment for the hair, giving it added body and shine.

Oil and skincare

Women through the ages have used oils made from local produce in their beauty regimes. Moroccans have used argan oil to keep their skin soft and supple for centuries, while Mediterraneans favour olive oil. Olive oil contains polyphenols, antioxidants that can help to slow down the ageing process, as well as preventing and repairing sun damage to the skin. Sweet almond oil is used in many skincare products; it is a very light oil which is easily absorbed into the skin. All vegetable oils contain vitamin E which is very good for the skin as it can help to reduce the appearance of scars, stretch marks and age spots. Oils can be gently massaged into the skin as they are, or can be used to make rich, moisturizing face packs and body lotions.

WHEATGERM OIL

Wheatgerm oil is rich in vitamin E and considered to be very good for the skin, although shouldn't be used by anyone with a wheat sensitivity.

For an intensive conditioning scalp treatment, warm 15ml/ 1 tbsp each of wheatgerm and olive oil and massage gently into the scalp. Wrap a warm towel around the head and leave for 10 minutes before rinsing off the oil.

Above: Oils can be fragranced with a few drops of a favourite essential oil.

Above: Any vegetable oil can be used for beauty treatments. Olive oil was traditionally used by the ancient Greeks and Romans; the Egyptians used scented almond oil.

Above: Argan oil is used by Moroccan women to keep their skin soft and smooth.

Above: Oil can be used to make nourishing body lotions and creams.

STORING BATH OILS

Home-made bath oils are best stored in coloured glass bottles, as exposure to light can cause the essential oils to deteriorate; plastic bottles should be avoided as the oils can react badly with the plastic.

Oil and cleansing

Bath oils are a wonderful beauty boon for those with dry skins. They float on the top of the water, and coat your entire body with a fine film when you step out of the bath. Ready-made bath oils are available, or use a few drops of any vegetable oil, such as olive, corn or groundnut (peanut) oil. Adding a few drops of a scented essential oil as well will give you a wonderfully fragrant bath.

Since the 6th century, French soap manufacturers have used olive oil to make their famous Marseilles soaps. Oils are also widely used in body scrubs and cleansers.

Oil and haircare

Any vegetable oil is suitable for conditioning the hair. Warm it slightly in the palm of your hand before massaging into the scalp. Wear a plastic shower cap for 20 minutes before shampooing and rinsing off the oil; the heat from your head will help the oil penetrate the hair shaft.

Above: Keep your favourite oils in the bathroom along with other beauty products.

OILS FOR BATHING

When combined with a blend of essential oils, bath oils can influence mood and health.
Olive oil soaps can be enriched with nut oils for a luxurious bathtime treat.

Seductive rose and sandalwood bath oil

Certain essential oils have an undeniably sensuous fragrance – this is certainly true of both rose and sandalwood essential oils. When combined with sandalwood oil, rose oil creates a warm, spicy aroma.

INGREDIENTS

100ml/3^1/$_2$ fl oz almond oil

20ml/4tsp wheatgerm oil

15 drops rose essential oil

10 drops sandalwood essential oil

1 Pour the almond oil and wheatgerm oil into an opaque glass bottle.

2 Add the rose and sandalwood essential oils and gently shake to mix.

3 Run a warm bath and add 15ml/ 1 tbsp of the oil to the water before you step in. Store in a cool, dark place and use within 1 year.

Beauty tip

Rose oil and sandalwood oil are costly to buy but a little will go a long way.

Milk and honey bath oil with rosemary

Milk is well known for its cleansing and lubricating qualities when applied to the skin. The addition of a little shampoo makes this a dispersing oil which does not leave a greasy rim around the bath.

INGREDIENTS

2 eggs

45ml/3 tbsp rosemary herb oil

10ml/2 tsp honey

10ml/2 tsp baby shampoo

15ml/1 tbsp vodka

150ml/^{1}/$_4$ pint/^{2}/$_3$ cup milk

1 Beat the eggs in a small bowl, then add the rosemary oil and mix.

2 Add the remaining ingredients to the bowl and mix together thoroughly.

3 Pour the bath oil into a clean opaque glass bottle.

4 Add 45ml/3 tbsp to the bath and keep the rest chilled, for use within a few days.

Grapefruit and coriander bath oil

A stimulating and refreshing combination of oils, this acts as a great reviver, especially when you are recovering from a cold or treating tired muscles after an exercise session at the gym.

INGREDIENTS

100ml/3^1/$_2$ fl oz almond oil

20ml/4tsp wheatgerm oil

30 drops grapefruit essential oil

30 drops coriander (cilantro) essential oil

1 Carefully pour the almond oil and wheatgerm oil into an opaque glass bottle.

2 Add the grapefruit and coriander essential oils and gently shake to mix.

3 Run a warm bath and add 15ml/ 1 tbsp of the oil to the water immediately before you step into the bath.

4 Store the bath oil in a cool, dark place and use within 1 year.

Olive oil and lavender soap

Enrich a block of naturally green Marseilles olive oil soap with nut oils and finely ground almonds and then scent it with lavender essential oil to make pretty guest soaps. Use heart-shaped moulds for a romantic touch.

INGREDIENTS

Makes about 4 soaps

175g/6oz Marseilles olive oil soap

25ml/1fl oz coconut oil

25ml/1fl oz almond oil

30ml/2 tbsp ground almonds

10 drops lavender essential oil

heart-shaped moulds, oiled

OLIVE OIL SOAP

Since the 6th century, French craftsmen have been making soaps from olive oil. The centre of soap production in France was Marseilles. Olive oil is rich in vitamin E, which helps the skin to retain moisture and remain bright and supple. Natural, unscented olive oil soaps are a great choice for cleansing sensitive skin.

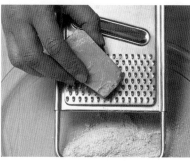

1 Grate the soap. Place the grated soap in a double boiler and leave it to soften over low heat. Add all the other ingredients.

2 Stir well, until all the ingredients are evenly mixed and begin to hold together.

3 Press the mixture into oiled moulds and leave to set overnight. Unmould the soaps and they are ready to use.

AN ANCIENT REMEDY

The ancient Greek physician Galen is said to have invented cold cream in the 2nd century AD. He did this by melting one part wax and adding three parts olive oil, then blending in as much water as the mixture would hold.

Marigold and sunflower soap

Make this sunny soap from unscented vegetable glycerine soap, adding nut oils, ground sunflower seeds and dried marigold petals.

INGREDIENTS

Makes about 4 soaps

175g/6oz vegetable glycerine soap

25ml/1fl oz coconut oil

25ml/1fl oz almond oil

30ml/2tbsp finely ground sunflower seeds

15ml/1tbsp dried marigold petals

10 drops bergamot essential oil

heart-shaped moulds, oiled

Make these soaps as for the olive oil and lavender soap. Use the same heart-shaped moulds, or try other shapes, if you like.

OILS FOR SOFT SKIN

From head to toe, different vegetable oils and essential oils can be used to make lotions, scrubs and creams to moisturize and condition the skin, leaving it soft and supple.

Soothing body polish

To soothe and polish rough skin, use lavender oil with bergamot, neroli or orange oil for a combination of relaxing and warming aromas.

INGREDIENTS

15ml/1 tbsp almond, avocado or
  macadamia oil
60ml/4 tbsp ground rice
lavender oil
bergamot, neroli or orange essential oil
mild body wash, to use

1 Place a little of the almond, avocado or macadamia oil in a small bowl.

2 Add enough ground rice to make a paste, and a few drops of the essential oils.

3 Before taking a shower, add a small amount of mild body wash and use on any areas of rough skin.

Beauty tip
Scrub from the middle outwards – stomach and down, then up and around the shoulders and arms.

Lavender body lotion

This creamy lotion is perfect for treating dry skin in winter. Borax is the salt of boric acid, known as sodium borate, sodium tetraborate or disodium tetraborate.

INGREDIENTS

1.5ml/$^1/_4$ tsp borax
5ml/1 tsp white beeswax
5ml/1 tsp lanolin
30ml/2 tbsp petroleum jelly
25ml/5 tsp plum seed oil
20ml/4 tsp cold pressed sunflower oil
20 drops lavender oil

1 Dissolve the borax in 30ml/2 tbsp boiled water. Melt the beeswax, lanolin and petroleum jelly with the plum seed and sunflower oil in a double boiler.

2 Remove from the heat once the wax has melted and stir well to blend. Add the borax solution while whisking. The lotion will turn white and thicken.

3 Whisk until cool Stir in the lavender oil. Pour into a glass bottle and store in a cool, dark place. Use within 1 year.

Traditional cold cream

This traditional, rose-scented cold cream has a light texture, which is quickly absorbed by the skin, leaving it feeling soft and pampered.

INGREDIENTS

50g/2oz white beeswax
120ml/4fl oz almond oil
50ml/2fl oz rosewater
2.5ml/$^1/_2$ tsp borax
120ml/4fl oz bottled spring water, heated

1 Melt the beeswax over a pan of hot water. Off the heat, whisk in the almond oil. Warm the rose water in a pan. Add the borax. Stir until it has dissolved.

2 Add the rosewater mixture to the hot spring water. Whisk into the melted wax and oil. It will start to emulsify, turning white and creamy. Whisk as the mixture cools, to ensure an even texture.

3 Spoon the cream into a jar and seal when it has completely cooled. Use within 6 months.

Coconut and orangeflower body lotion

This creamy preparation is wonderfully nourishing for dry skin. Wheatgerm oil is rich in vitamin E, an antioxidant that protects skin cells against premature ageing.

INGREDIENTS

50g/2 oz coconut oil

60ml/4 tbsp sunflower oil

10ml/2 tsp wheatgerm oil

10 drops orangeflower essence or 5 drops
  neroli essential oil

1 Melt the coconut oil in a bowl over gently simmering water. Stir in the sunflower and wheatgerm oils.

2 Leave to cool, then add the fragrance and pour into a jar. The lotion will solidify after several hours. Store in a cool, dark place and use within 6 months.

YOUNGER SKIN

Massage the skin with a mixture of equal parts olive oil and lemon juice to help prevent wrinkles forming.

Olive oil body scrub

INGREDIENTS

120ml/4 fl oz/½ cup olive oil

30ml/2tbsp sea salt

Mix the ingredients together in a small bowl. Take a shower and, while your skin is still wet, rub the mixture over your body (avoiding any areas of broken skin). Rinse off thoroughly.

INEXPENSIVE BODY LOTION

Instead of expensive body lotions, use aqueous cream BP, which is mild and unscented. (It is often recommended by pharmacists and medics for soothing irritated skins and mild rashes.) Transfer a little of the cream (it is usually sold in large pots) to a small sterilized pot and mix in a few drops of essential oil. Prepare a calming mixture for evening and an invigorating one for day. Massage a little macadamia or avocado oil over the skin first, then rub in the cream, which will help the skin to absorb the oil.

OILS FOR HAND TREATMENTS

Oils soften and moisturize the skin and improve the condition of the nails and cuticles. Sweet almond and macadamia are good for their light aromas but olive oil is also very effective.

Winter hand cream

This is a very nourishing cream incorporating patchouli oil, which is a particularly good healer of cracked and chapped skin. Follow the traditional treatment for sore hands by covering them in a generous layer of cream last thing at night and then pulling on a pair of soft cotton gloves. Your hands will have absorbed the cream by morning.

INGREDIENTS

75g/3oz unscented, hard white soap

115g/4oz beeswax

45ml/3 tbsp glycerine

150ml/^{1}/4 pint/^{2}/3 cup almond oil

45ml/3 tbsp rose water

25 drops patchouli oil

1 Grate the unscented soap and place it in a bowl. Pour over 90ml/6 tbsp boiling water and stir until smooth.

2 Combine the beeswax, glycerine, almond oil and rose water in a double boiler then melt over a gentle heat.

3 Remove from the heat and gradually whisk in the soap mixture. Keep whisking as the mixture cools and thickens.

4 Stir in the patchouli oil and pour into a jar. Store in a cool, dark place. use within 1 year.

Natural nail polish

After trimming and tidying your nails, use oils to condition them.

Soak nails in a little olive oil for 5 minutes, then exfoliate the hands with an oil-based face scrub. Rinse, then polish nails with two or three grades of polishing board and leather. Use a little macadamia or sweet almond oil with the fine grade polisher.

HANDY TIPS

• Massage a little oil and cream into the hands before starting gardening or any other work that is hard on the hands. Tea tree oil is good to massage in with some hand cream before wearing rubber gloves or gardening gloves.

• Rub a little olive oil into your fingernails each night before you go to bed, to stop them chipping and flaking.

Hand cream plus

Using hand cream with oils will promote the absorption of the oil.

Massage a little macadamia nut oil into the hands before using your usual hand cream. Add a drop of essential oil to each hand last thing at night or before relaxing.

OILS FOR FOOTCARE

The moisturizing properties of oil can also be used on the feet, where the skin (especially on the heel area or the side of the big toe) can be dry or rough.

Easy oil pedicure

Regularly using a refreshing peppermint, eucalyptus and lemon scrub on the feet will keep them soft. Using crushed rice or sea salt will remove any rough or hard skin.

INGREDIENTS

5ml/1 tsp peppermint oil

5ml/1 tsp eucalytpus oil

5ml/1 tsp lemon oil

15ml/1 tbsp olive oil

60ml/4 tbsp crushed rice or sea salt

100ml/3¹/₂fl oz/scant 1 cup avocado, almond or macadamia oil

1 Start by filing nails to length with an emery board before softening up the skin.

2 Soak the feet in hot soapy water with a few drops of the peppermint oil added.

3 Combine the crushed rice or sea salt with a little olive oil and a drop each of the peppermint, eucalyptus and lemon oils.

4 Use to scrub the feet, concentrating on any areas of rough skin. Wash off the scrub, then rinse the feet in warm water mixed with a drop of peppermint oil.

5 To finish, massage avocado, almond or macadamia oil into the nails and cuticles.

FOOT HEALTH

• Anti-fungal and antiseptic oils are excellent for preventing foot odours or worse problems, and also for helping to treat them. Tea tree oil and vinegar are both helpful and they can be combined with olive oil to make a soothing and cleansing rub. Apply generously to the feet and wrap in clear film (plastic wrap), then leave for about 20 minutes to soak in.

• Alternatively, use this combination of ingredients in a foot soak.

• Add tea tree oil to base oil for a massage or to aqueous cream BP with a little peppermint for a lotion. Always thoroughly dry between the toes.

• To avoid picking up infections, wear flip-flops when using communal swimming pools, showers and other wet areas in public facilities.

Foot pack

Applying a rejuvenating pack to run-down feet works wonders.

Combine beneficial fruit or vegetable purées with a nourishing oil, such as almond, avocado or olive oil. Wrap the feet in cling film (plastic wrap), enclose in a warm towel and leave to work wonders for 30 minutes.

Foot lotions

Use soothing essential oils on tired feet.

Add a few drops of peppermint or eucalyptus oil to a bottle of body lotion – aqueous cream BP is suitable or use a standard body lotion. For a cooling treat for tired feet, smoothe a little eucalyptus oil into the feet, then massage in witch hazel gel.

OILS FOR HAIRCARE

Essential oils are very good for the hair – rosemary promotes great hair condition, especially for darker hair colours. Camomile is used in treatments for fair hair and to help balance greasy hair.

Essential oil shampoo

Mix up small quantities of shampoo or conditioner using a favourite essential oil, such as rose, lavender, bergamot (good for oily hair) or palmarosa.

INGREDIENTS

shampoo or conditioner
2.5ml/¹/₂ tsp essential oil

1 Pour shampoo or conditioner into small travel bottles (or rinsed-out hotel bottles) and add a few drops of oil.

2 Mix with a plastic or stainless steel swizzle stick or skewer.

Variation

Make all-in-one shampoo and conditioner by pouring a favourite shampoo into a small bottle. Add a thin layer of conditioner on top of the shampoo and a few drops of rosemary and palmarosa oil (or another combination of favourite oils).

Dry hair conditioning treatment

Egg yolk is naturally rich in vitamins and when mixed with olive oil will work wonders to improve the health and appearance of dry lifeless hair.

INGREDIENTS

1 egg yolk
120ml/4fl oz/¹/₂ cup olive oil
2 drops lavender essential oil

1 Beat the egg yolk and gradually add the olive oil, then the lavender oil.

2 Massage the egg and oil mixture into your hair and scalp.

3 Soak a towel in hot water, wring it out so that it is damp rather than wet and wrap it around your hair.

4 Leave the treatment in your hair for at least an hour before shampooing, rinsing thoroughly.

Essential oil hair rinse

Mix a favourite essential oil with cider vinegar and rose or orange flower water to remove product build-up from the hair. Try jojoba oil for damaged hair.

INGREDIENTS

30ml/2 tbsp cider vinegar
90ml/6 tbsp rosewater or orange flower water
2 drops essential oil, such as jojoba

1 Mix one quarter cider vinegar to three quarters rosewater or orange flower water in a small container.

2 Add 2 drops of the chosen essential oil. After shampooing and conditioning as usual, rinse your hair.

3 Sprinkle a little of the oil and vinegar hair rinse over the wet hair and massage thoroughly.

4 Gently rinse off the hair.

Rosemary massage treatment

Massage is excellent for promoting circulation and a healthy scalp. Try this super-conditioning three-stage treatment for regenerating tired hair that is dry and lacking in shine. Rosemary is particularly good for dark hair colours.

Honey and oil conditioner

Add softness and shine to dry hair with honey and olive oil.

INGREDIENTS

45ml/3 tbsp clear honey

120ml/4fl oz/$^1/_2$ cup olive oil

2 drops rosemary essential oil

15ml/1 tbsp cider vinegar

1 Mix the honey with the olive oil and add the rosemary essential oil.

2 Massage the mixture into your hair and wrap a hot, damp towel around it.

3 Leave the conditioner on your hair for at least an hour before shampooing and rinsing thoroughly, adding the cider vinegar to the water for the final rinse to make the hair shine.

INGREDIENTS

mild washing up liquid

6 drops rosemary oil

15 ml/1 tbsp jojoba oil

mild shampoo

good-quality unscented or tea
  tree conditioner

1 Begin by brushing the hair well, working very gently so as not to stretch or break the hair at all.

2 Brush the hair in all directions, first brushing it out to ensure it is not tangled, then turning the head upside down. Finally, brush from first one side, then the other.

3 Use a little mild washing up liquid to wash the hair thoroughly, working up a good lather gently without too much excessive rubbing. Take care to avoid tangling or stretching the hair. Rinse the soap off with warm water.

4 Mix 3 drops of rosemary oil into the jojoba oil and massage into the scalp.

5 Begin by distributing through the hair evenly. Then work the fingertips from the sides (above the ears) up and over the top of the head, crossing in the middle. Next work from front to top and back to top in the same way, crossing the fingers on top of the head.

6 Repeat until the oil is thoroughly distributed, lifting the fingers out and away from the head, and through the hair, each time they cross on top.

7 Wash the hair with a mild shampoo to remove the oil.

8 Mix 2–3 drops rosemary oil into a small amount of the unscented or tea tree conditioner, then gently massage this through the hair. Leave for about 30 seconds before rinsing off.

Camomile and bergamot wash and rinse

This is a very good treatment for fair hair that has a tendency to be greasy.

INGREDIENTS

250ml/8fl oz/1 cup strong camomile tea

3–4 drops bergamot oil

1 Brew a mug of strong camomile tea, preferably with dried camomile flowers and boiling water. Leave to infuse until completely cold, then strain into a jug (pitcher).

2 Add the bergamot oil to the camomile tea. Gently work shampoo into the scalp as usual. Before creating the usual foam, gradually add about a third of the camomile and bergamot water.

3 Continue washing as usual, rinse and condition. Rinse the conditioner off. Finally, rinse the hair with the remaining camomile and bergamot liquid.

Intensive hot oil conditioning

This is great for anyone with a dry scalp or dry or colour-damaged hair.

INGREDIENTS

45ml/3 tbsp olive oil

mild shampoo

30ml/2 tbsp cider vinegar

1 Rinse a cup with boiling water to warm it before pouring in 45 ml/3 tbsp olive oil. Stand the cup in a bowl of boiling water to heat the oil.

2 Place a towel to heat on a radiator. Have a roll of cling film (plastic wrap) ready. Wash the hair with a cleansing shampoo or a little detergent, if necessary, to remove any product build-up.

3 Massage the hot oil through the hair, fingering the scalp all over and working the oil out to the ends of the hair.

4 Work the hair up neatly around the head and wrap it all tightly in clear film. Then wrap in a hot towel and relax for 15–30 minutes.

5 Use a mild shampoo to wash out the oil. Massage 30 ml/2 tbsp cider vinegar through the hair and rinse thoroughly.

HAIRCARE TIP

Decant favourite everyday shampoo and conditioner into small bottles and add a few drops of lavender oil. The oil will impart a pleasant, relaxing aroma.

Overnight lavender treatment

This is an excellent way of benefiting from lavender oil, which will promote a good night's sleep while calming stressed, dry hair. Begin the treatment 2–3 hours before going to bed to avoid having wet hair on the pillow.

INGREDIENTS

3 drops of lavender oil

30 ml/2 tbsp olive oil

1 Wash the hair and towel it dry, then gently comb out any tangles.

2 Mix 3 drops of lavender oil into 30 ml/2 tbsp olive oil and massage this through the hair, working it into the scalp and out through the hair.

3 Gently comb the oil through and leave the hair to dry naturally, rubbing with a towel occasionally.

4 Protect your pillow with a towel to avoid staining or damage. The following morning, wash off with a mild shampoo, then rinse and condition lightly as usual.

Beauty tip

Lavender oil can be used as an effective treatment against head lice.

Hair rescuer

When regularly exposed to the elements, hair can become dry and unmanageable. Central heating, air conditioning and cold weather can all affect the hair's condition. This is a rich nourishing formula, to help improve the condition of dry and damaged hair.

INGREDIENTS

30ml/2tbsp olive oil

30ml/2tbsp light sesame oil

2 eggs

30ml/2tbsp coconut milk

30ml/2tbsp runny honey

5ml/1tsp coconut oil

blender or food processor

1 Place all of the ingredients together in the blender or food processor and process until smooth.

2 Carefully transfer the treatment to a suitable container.

3 After shampooing as usual, comb the mixture through your hair, ensuring even coverage. Leave in the hair for about 5 minutes and then rinse out with warm water.

4 Keep refrigerated and use within three days.

Perk-up conditioner

This makes a zingy conditioner for morning hair washing.

Pour 50ml/2 fl oz/$^1/_4$ cup good-quality mild hair conditioner into a small container. Add 1 drop each of rosemary, tea tree and eucalyptus oil to the conditioner and mix together well.

Coconut oil treatment

Using this treatment once a month will work wonders for your hair and scalp.

Mix 90ml/6tbsp coconut oil with 3 drops rosemary oil, 2 drops tea tree oil and 2 drops lavender oil. Use the oil sparingly on dry hair. Coat the hair rather than saturate it, and gently massage it in. Cover with a hot towel for 20 minutes, then shampoo off.

OILS FOR FACIAL SKINCARE

Use milder oils for the delicate skin on the face. Macadamia nut oil is a good choice, but sweet almond oil, wheatgerm oil, avocado oil and olive oil will all benefit dry skin.

5 Gently pat the face dry with a towel and rinse it all over with a mixture of equal quantities witch hazel and rosewater.

Scrub and soothe session

This is a deep cleansing treat, starting with a scrub, followed with a macadamia and palmarosa mask that rounds off to a gentle polish. Salt is thoroughly cleansing but it is harsh – for sensitive skin use the rice flour scrub.

For the scrub

5ml/1 tsp salt

5ml/1 tsp honey

5ml/1 tsp rolled oats or 5ml/1 tsp rice flour

For the freshener

witch hazel

rosewater

For the smoothing mask

5ml/1 tsp macadamia nut oil

10 ml/2 tsp rice flour

2–3 drops palmarosa oil

To finish

2 drops palmarosa oil

5ml/1 tsp macadamia nut oil

1 Mix 5 ml/1 tsp each of salt, honey and rolled oats. (Alternatively, use the honey, oats and 2.5–5ml/½–1 tsp rice flour for sensitive skin.)

2 Add a few drops of water to slacken the salt mixture – do not add much or it will become very runny as too much salt dissolves.

3 Gently apply the mixture to the face, avoiding the eye area. Rub lightly only around the nose and chin area and over the forehead. Avoid the lips and eyes, and do not scrub the delicate skin on the cheeks – simply smooth the mixture over the skin.

4 Leave the mixture on the face for 5 minutes. Then wash off, scrubbing gently around the nose and chin.

6 To make the smoothing mask, mix 5 ml/1 tsp macadamia nut oil with about 10 ml/2 tsp rice flour, mixing in just enough to make a smooth, thin paste. Mix in 2-3 drops palmarosa oil.

7 Spread this over the face avoiding the eye area. Leave for 15–30 minutes. Rinse off the mask with lukewarm water, rubbing gently. Pat dry and rinse with witch hazel and rosewater or freshener as before.

8 Mix 2 drops palmarosa oil into 5 ml/1 tsp macadamia nut oil and smooth a little over the face with the tips of the fingers.

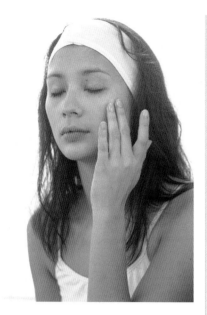

Comfrey and rosewater mask

Herbal face masks tighten the skin, leaving it smooth and fresh. They help to heal blemishes, refine open pores, nourish and soothe. It is best not to use them too often as they can be over-stimulating. This mask is ideal for nourishing dry skin.

INGREDIENTS

6 comfrey leaves
150ml/¹/4 pint/²/3 cup boiling water
30ml/2 tbsp fine oatmeal
1 egg yolk
5ml/1 tsp honey
5ml/1 tsp rosewater
5 drops wheatgerm oil
a little milk or yogurt to mix

1 Infuse the comfrey leaves in the boiling water and leave to cool.

2 Strain the infusion into a small bowl.

3 Mix 15ml/1 tbsp of this infusion with the other ingredients to make a smooth paste.

4 Apply evenly to the face, avoiding the eye area. Leave for 10–15 minutes, then rinse off with warm water.

Almond oil cleanser

This almond oil cleanser is a traditional mixture of beeswax, almond oil and rosewater. All creams and lotions are emulsions of oils and water and the addition of a tiny amount of borax means that this mixture emulsifies in a moment, forming a silky-smooth, creamy lotion worthy of the best cosmetic houses. Add essential oils, if you like. Rose oil is suitable for all skin types, and frankincense is particularly good for older skin. To use, smooth it on to the skin using a gentle circular movement and remove with damp cotton wool.

INGREDIENTS

25g/1oz white beeswax
150ml/5fl oz almond oil
1.5ml/¹/4 tsp borax (available from chemists)
60ml/4tbsp rosewater
2 drops rose or frankincense essential
  oil (optional)

1 Melt the beeswax in a double boiler and whisk in the almond oil.

2 In a pan, add the borax to the rosewater and warm gently, to dissolve.

3 Slowly add the rosewater mixture to the oils, whisking all the time.

4 Add the essential oil, if using. The mixture will quickly emulsify. Whisk until the mixture has a smooth, creamy texture.

5 Pour into the container, leave to cool and replace the lid securely. Store in a cool, dark place and use within 3 months.

Super-rich avocado face mask

Avocado has been valued as a beauty ingredient for thousands of years. It was used in skincare regimes by the Maya, Aztecs and Incas. The fruit is rich in beneficial oils that will brighten and moisturize tired-looking skin.

INGREDIENTS

150ml/^{1}/4 pint/^{2}/3 cup olive oil

1 large avocado

1 Peel the avocado and remove the stone (pit). Roughly chop the flesh, place in a small bowl and mash with a fork.

2 Pour enough of the olive oil over the avocado to make a smooth paste and mix together thoroughly.

3 Apply to the face and leave on the skin for at least 15–20 minutes before rinsing off with warm water.

Gentle almond face scrub

This is a face scrub worthy of Cleopatra, with its luxurious blend of almonds, oatmeal, milk and rose petals. The rose petals should be bought from an herbalist or, if you want to use petals from your garden, be sure that they have not been sprayed with chemicals. The rose petals can be powdered in a pestle and mortar or in an electric coffee grinder. When mixed with almond oil, the scrub will cleanse the face and leave it silky-soft.

INGREDIENTS

45ml/3 tbsp ground almonds

45ml/3 tbsp medium oatmeal

45ml/3 tbsp powdered milk

30ml/2 tbsp powdered rose petals, or rose oil

30ml/2 tbsp almond oil

1 Mix the ingredients together in a bowl and transfer to a glass jar. Stored in a cool, dark place, the scrub will keep for 1 year.

2 Before using, mix a small amount of the scrub with enough of the almond oil to make a soft paste.

3 Gently rub the scrub into the skin, using a circular motion and being careful to avoid the delicate area around the eyes.

4 Rinse off with warm water and pat your face dry.

Avocado and lemon mask

This rich mask is both moisturizing and refreshing when applied to the face.

INGREDIENTS

1 avocado
5ml/1 tsp lemon juice
5ml/1 tsp avocado oil
cornflour (corn starch), optional

1 Carefully peel the avocado and remove the stone (pit).

2 Purée or sieve (strain) the avocado flesh and stir or whisk in 5ml/1 tsp each of lemon juice and avocado oil.

3 If the mixture seems too runny, sprinkle in a little cornflour to thicken it slightly to a spreading paste.

4 Cleanse the skin thoroughly and then spread the mask over your face, avoiding the delicate eye area.

5 Relax for 15–20 minutes before washing off the mask with warm water.

Beauty tips

Do not use face masks on sore or broken skin. If you have sensitive skin, it is advisable to perform a patch test first on a small area of skin.

Cleansing mask for blackheads

Lemon juice contains natural fruit acids that are beneficial for the skin.

INGREDIENTS

30ml/2 tbsp oatmeal
30ml/2 tbsp yogurt
15ml/1 tbsp lemon juice
15ml/1 tbsp olive oil

1 Place all the ingredients in a small bowl and mix well to make a paste,

2 Smooth the mask over the face.

3 Leave for 10 minutes, then rinse off with cool water.

WHICH OILS TO USE?

• The most useful oils for promoting skin regeneration and general good condition are macadamia nut oil and avocado oil.

• Sweet almond oil is mild, and easily absorbed by the skin and so very good to use in home-made face treatments.

• Geranium, lavender, neroli, orange, palmarosa, rose and rosewood essential oils are all ideal for use in many skin potions, including oil mixtures intended as occasional intensive moisturizers.

Facial mask for dry skin

The vitamins in the egg yolk will add moisture to dry skin.

INGREDIENTS

1 egg yolk
15ml/1 tbsp olive oil
5ml/1 tsp lemon juice

1 Beat the egg yolk in a small bowl and add the olive oil gradually.

2 Add a few drops of lemon juice.

3 Smooth the mixture on to your face and leave until dry, then rinse off with warm water.

Moisturizer aromas

Revitalize a pot of cream that is half used and beginning to lose its fragrance.

Add a few drops of a favourite essential oil to the moisturizer or night cream and mix.

OILS IN THE HOME AND GARDEN

The oils used in cooking may be the most familiar, but there are also non-edible oils that are used around the home. From restoring and protecting furniture to cleaning metals, lubricating rusting hinges and taking care of shoes, it is worth trying some of these traditional materials and methods, instead of relying on commercial products. Using simple techniques and mixtures that have been passed down through generations is satisfying and the results are often a brilliant surprise.

Left: Tung oil and walnut oil are among the oils which may be used around the house for treating wood, lubrication, cleaning or polishing.

USING OILS AROUND THE HOME

The culinary vegetable oils can be put to many good uses outside of the kitchen, but non-edible oils are more suited to tough household jobs.

Oils that are produced for household use do not have to be extracted and processed through a food-safe environment or to the same standards that remove natural toxins. While the following may also be found among culinary oils, the hardware store equivalents are not safe for consumption. The edible kitchen versions of these oils can be put to use around the home, but are usually more expensive.

Useful non-edible oils

Linseed oil This is available from hardware suppliers and is a non-edible product that is reserved for household use, particularly for cleaning and protecting wood. It is essential to distinguish between ordinary or raw linseed oil and boiled linseed oil. Raw linseed oil will not dry to the same extent as boiled linseed oil. It will be absorbed but if an excess is applied it will not dry to a fine glaze but will become very sticky.

Boiled linseed oil was traditionally prepared by heating to 210–260°C/410–500°F, sometimes with additional ingredients to promote drying. Blown oil is processed by blowing hot air through it rather than heating in the traditional way. Artists' materials include linseed oils with different drying times, to slow down the drying time of the paint, retard it completely or to speed up the drying time.

Olive oil Non-edible grade olive oil is known as 'lampante' and was traditionally used as a lamp oil. It is common sense that using expensive extra virgin or virgin olive oils for household uses such as polishing tables or to prevent a hinge from squeaking is not sensible but ordinary olive oil can certainly be used for polishing and restoring.

Poppy seed oil This is used in artists' painting products and sold for mixing with paint as a slow-drying medium.

Teak oil This is a blend of oils with excellent drying properties. It is used to treat wood, protecting its surface and enhancing its appearance.

Tung oil This is obtained from the seeds of the tung tree, varieties of which are native to China and Japan.

Above: A varnish will form a protective coating on top of wood, but when wood is treated with boiled linseed oil, the oil soaks into the surface, leaving a shiny finish and emphasizing the natural grain of the wood.

Above: Mix cedar oil with beeswax, turpentine and sandalwood essential oil to make a fragrant furniture polish.

Above: 'Lampante' olive oil is useful for cleaning metal objects.

Above: Oils can be used as a treatment for wood both in the home and the garden.

Above: Teak has a rich golden colour. Over time, items of teak furniture will gradually fade. To prolong the natural colour, the wood should be sanded and treated with teak oil.

It is also referred to as wood oil or Chinese or Japanese wood oil. The oil has excellent drying properties and it is used in artists' materials as well as for treating wood. Being non-toxic, pure tung oil is sold for treating kitchen surfaces, including chopping boards. (Always double check the manufacturer's information to ensure that the particular oil is produced to non-toxic standards before applying it to cooking surfaces.)

Walnut oil This is a good drying oil and one that was traditionally used by artists as a paint thinner and brush cleaner. Walnut oil was preferred to linseed oil as it was less likely to crack or craze when drying.

Cedar oil This oil is made from the cedar tree and has a long history of being used around the home. It formed the base for paints used by the ancient Sumerians. Today, cedar oil is often used in aromatherapy. It can also be used as a floor polish and an insect repellent. A little cedar oil applied to natural cedar furniture will help to renew the lovely woody aroma.

Some uses for oils

There are many ways that these oils can be used around the home and in the garden. Mixtures based on linseed oil can be used to polish and treat wood. Oils are useful in floor polishes and for cleaning and feeding leather, including shoes.

Applying a small amount of oil to an object made from metals such as copper, bronze or brass will provide a barrier between the object and the air and will prevent tarnishing. Using oil in the garden to treat wooden furniture will help it to withstand the elements. A few drops of the right oil will ease stiff hinges, locks or even tools.

A little boiled linseed oil can even be used in the restoration of oil paintings, although great care should be taken to avoid causing damage.

OILS FOR POLISHING AND CLEANING

Before spray polish took over, many people mixed their own potions using oil as a base. Professional restorers still have their favourite mixtures for restoring antique furniture.

Furniture reviver

Wooden surfaces can become grimy from a combination of dirt and a build-up of spray polish. Use this traditional country recipe to loosen the grime and feed the wood at the same time.

INGREDIENTS

250ml/8fl oz/1 cup malt vinegar

250ml/8fl oz/1 cup pure turpentine

250ml/8fl oz/1 cup raw linseed oil

15ml/1 tbsp sugar

1 Measure all the ingredients into a bottle with a cork or screw top, seal and shake well to mix.

2 Label the bottle clearly.

3 Used over a few weeks, this will gradually remove the layers of polish. Apply with a soft cloth, leave for a few minutes, then wipe off with a second cloth.

Furniture oil

This furniture oil traditionally included benzoin, a resin obtained from an East Indian tree of the same name. It would have been sold in hardware stores a century ago but experimenting today means improvising. The common tincture of benzoin was better known as Friar's Balsam, a product that is still available today from pharmacies or chemist shops. It gives the polish a powerful and refreshing aroma.

INGREDIENTS

200ml/7fl oz/scant 1 cup vinegar

200ml/7fl oz/scant 1 cup boiled linseed oil

25g/1oz benzoin or Friar's Balsam

1 Pour the vinegar, boiled linseed oil and benzoin into an airtight jar.

2 Screw the lid on tight and shake until the mixture is thoroughly combined. Apply to furniture with a soft cloth.

Linseed and shellac polish

Shellac is sold as dry flakes or dissolved in alcohol as liquid shellac varnish. It is a traditional wood finish.

Warm 150ml/$\frac{1}{4}$ pint/$\frac{2}{3}$ cup boiled linseed oil and 7g/$\frac{1}{3}$oz shellac varnish in a small bowl placed over hot water. Stir well to combine. Remove from the heat and allow to cool before using to polish wooden furniture.

TEST PATCH

Furniture polishes should always be tested on a small area first. Absorbent surfaces will change colour when treated with oil-based mixtures. Leather and wood will darken and marks that were insignificant on a dried-out surface may become more prominent. These types of mixtures are ideal for restoring old pieces of furniture, especially less-expensive items that look rather sad and neglected. They are useful for raw wood but not for use on varnished or lacquered modern furniture.

Beeswax and turpentine polish

This is a very simple polish to make and the addition of wood oils will give it an attractive resinous fragrance. Lemon or lavender essential oil may also be used in this polish. Apply to your furniture using a soft cloth, leave a few minutes to dry, then buff vigorously with a soft duster to achieve a deep, lustrous shine.

INGREDIENTS

75g/3oz natural beeswax

200ml/7fl oz/³/4 cup pure turpentine

20 drops cedar oil

10 drops sandalwood oil

1 Grate the beeswax coarsely and place in a screw-top jar.

2 Pour on the turpentine, seal, and leave for a week, stirring occasionally until the mixture becomes a smooth cream.

3 Add the essential oils and mix them in well. The polish is then ready to use.

RENOVATING TIPS

Oil mixtures are ideal for reviving dirty items of furniture, removing years of grime and restoring a shine to old polished surfaces. Use a soft, clean, lint-free cloth to work in the chosen mixture. Work with the grain of the wood, rubbing in the oil or polish along it, not across it, then allow it to soak in or dry before polishing off later. The surface may be rubbed with fine sandpaper and a little boiled linseed oil after the first polish, then left to dry and wiped with a cloth lightly moistened with vinegar before applying more of the oil-based polish.

On untreated wood, some of the best satin finishes that bring out the beauty of light woods are built up over time by cleaning occasionally with a simple mixture that soaks in. Unlike spray polishes that leave a film on the surface, oil-based cleaners feed the wood.

When working on old or damaged furniture, first inspect for woodworm attack and treat the wood accordingly if needed. Then repair any structural damage or wear. Remove surface damage by cleaning and sanding, taking care not to inflict further damage. Old polish or lacquer should be removed by scraping, rubbing down with emery paper and cleaning with white vinegar to provide a smooth, clean surface.

When you are preparing any potentially toxic (and flammable) mixtures, use containers that will not be used for food in future. Heat mixtures carefully, using low heat and taking particular care to avoid direct contact with a naked flame – a heatproof container over a pan of hot water is usually the best way. Always work in a well-ventilated place when handling mixtures that produce strong odours.

Removing marks from furniture

This is a traditional country remedy for cleaning and protecting furniture. The oily mixture will form a light barrier on the surface of the wood, helping to keep it relatively unmarked by fingers. Remember to test the polish on a small area that is out of sight before using on precious items of furniture.

INGREDIENTS

2.4 litres/4 pints water
40g/1¹/₂oz soap flakes
15ml/1 tbsp olive oil

1 Place the water in a large bowl and add the soap flakes.

2 Mix thoroughly with a wooden spoon until the soap flakes have completely dissolved.

3 Add the olive oil and stir until thoroughly combined.

4 Dip a clean cloth into the mixture, wring out any excess liquid, and carefully wipe the piece of furniture all over with the mixture.

5 Dry the furniture thoroughly with a clean, dry cloth.

Non-slip polish for floors

This traditional mixture was intended to be non-slip but it is worth remembering that any polished floors are slippery unless they are made from contemporary products and finishes. There are many variations on the mixture of the popular polishing materials of oil, vinegar and turpentine.

INGREDIENTS

475ml/16fl oz/2 cups white vinegar
475ml/16fl oz/2 cups turpentine
475ml/16fl oz/2 cups boiled linseed oil

1 Place the vinegar, turpentine and boiled linseed oil in an airtight jar.

2 Shake well until the mixture is thoroughly combined.

3 Rub the mixture over the floor with a cloth and leave to dry. Do not buff the floor – this will make it slippery

CLEANING STAINLESS STEEL

Use a small amount of olive oil on a cloth to polish stainless steel surfaces – this will leave them shiny and streak-free. This also works on stainless steel sinks in the kitchen.

Polish for fine scratches

Use this method for minor scratches, otherwise professional polishing is best.

Rub a little walnut oil over a fine scratch, preferably as soon as it is noticed. This will help to restore the colour to the wood and make scratches less noticeable.

Olive oil polish

This is a very simple polish. Use it to clean up pieces of wooden furniture.

Pour equal parts of turpentine and olive oil into a jar with an airtight lid and shake until thoroughly combined. Use to clean and polish furniture, rubbing it over evenly following the grain of the wood. Then polish off with a clean cloth.

Cleaning linoleum

Linoleum (or 'lino') flooring was traditionally cleaned with linseed oil, which restored the colour, protected the surface and kept the flooring in good condition.

Use boiled linseed oil and rub it in well, then polish it off. The result will be a gleaming floor; however, it will also be extremely slippery! Alternatively, mix equal parts of turpentine and olive oil in a small jar, then add a little warm milk and shake well. Use this to clean linoleum or oilcloth.

WEIGHING AND MEASURING

When using mixtures that are toxic, it is important to make sure they do not contaminate equipment that will be used for cooking. Keep a separate mixing spoon, bowl and jug. Pack them away in a separate place (not in the kitchen) after use.

Airtight jars are ideal for the majority of mixing, and precision is not usually vital. Some of the mixtures suggest quantities but it is often a good idea to mix a little in a small jar, judging the proportions by eye, to experiment. If necessary, use electronic kitchen scales on which the bowl or jar can stand.

Cleaning and feeding leather

Olive or other vegetable oil can be used to ease surface dirt off leather. This works well on old briefcases or handbags, suitcases and similar items.

INGREDIENTS
120ml/4 fl oz/$^{1}/_{2}$ cup olive oil
120ml/4 fl oz/$^{1}/_{2}$ cup white vinegar
boiled linseed oil

1 Use a fairly generous amount of oil on a clean, lint-free cloth to gently rub off dirt and feed the leather.

2 Then rub the leather with a little white vinegar on another clean cloth. Leave to dry before finally treating with a mixture of equal parts olive oil and white vinegar.

3 Polish off with a clean cloth.

4 Alternatively, leather upholstery can be cleaned and its texture preserved by rubbing occasionally with a mixture of one part vinegar to two parts boiled linseed oil. The mixture should be used very sparingly.

OILS FOR CLEANING METALS

A little oil can be used on polishing cloths for metals such as copper, bronze or brass, to form a light barrier between the metal and air, and help to minimize tarnishing.

Copper polish

Soft metals such as copper need very careful cleaning. Applying a thin coating of olive oil after cleaning will protect the metal and prevent tarnishing.

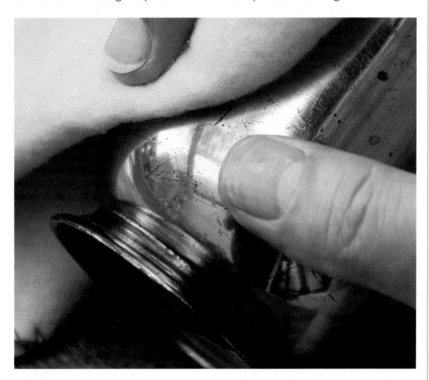

Bronze cleaner

Use sweet almond oil plus linseed oil to clean bronze items.

Rub the metal thoroughly with sweet almond oil. Polish off the oil with a clean cloth. Use a small soft brush to clean intricate areas. For really hard-to-clean metal, linseed oil can be used and cleaned off first. Then polish the bronze with sweet almond oil and rub with a chamois leather.

INGREDIENTS

a pinch of salt

1 lemon

15ml/1 tbsp olive oil

1 Sprinkle a pinch of salt on to a saucer. Cut the lemon in half. Take one half and dip the cut surface in the salt. Rub the salty lemon over the copper.

2 Rinse the item in clean hot water and dry immediately with a clean cloth.

3 Place a little olive oil on a clean cloth and rub this over the item before finishing with a clean cloth. To maintain a shine, give the metal an occasional rub with a cloth moistened with olive oil and then polish it off.

Brass cleaner

Use oil on brass to create a barrier between the brass and the air.

After polishing brass items, rub with a cloth dipped in a little olive oil. This will help to prevent tarnishing as well as making it gleam.

OILS IN THE GARDEN

Oil, particularly linseed oil, is well-known for its wood-preserving properties. These can be put to good use on garden furniture that must be treated in order to withstand the elements.

Outdoor wood preservation

Boiled linseed oil is a brilliant wood preservative, especially for sheds or summerhouses that are south-facing and exposed to summer sun, which makes the wood dry out and shrink. The wood must be completely dry and it is best to do this on a warm, but not hot, day and early on in the day so that the oil has time to dry before evening. Applying the oil in hot blazing sun is not ideal as it does not allow for maximum absorption.

Hardwood furniture treatment

Teak oil is best for hardwood furniture, but boiled linseed oil can be used instead.

Rub furniture down with fine sandpaper to loosen the surface and ensure the oil is absorbed. Treat furniture with teak oil regularly and use a cloth dipped in an oil and vinegar mixture (ordinary vegetable oil) to wipe off dust and dirt rather than soapy water.

INGREDIENTS

75ml/5 tbsp boiled linseed oil

1 Thoroughly rub down the wood, first with a brush to remove any loose dirt, then with sandpaper to remove any residue of old surface treatment. Use a wire brush to rub off tough dirt, taking care not to scratch the wood.

2 Rub again with emery paper and brush off with a soft brush.

3 Brush boiled linseed oil generously into the wood, working with the grain and brushing into, under and around joins. Leave to dry for a day or so and then apply a second coat. Treat wood every year and it will last a lifetime!

Greenhouse treatment

This is good for faded and dried out wood as it will absorb a large quantity of oil.

Mix equal parts boiled linseed oil and sunflower oil, and brush on for a first coat. Thoroughly clean, brush down and rub the wood with sandpaper, then brush off all dust and debris. This will bring the wood back to life. Apply a second coat of undiluted boiled linseed oil. This will dry to protect the wood.

OILS FOR LUBRICATION

Every household should have a handy can of light general purpose oil for simple everyday tasks, such as oiling a squeaky hinge or loosening a stiff lock.

Locks

Padlocks or outdoor locks on garden sheds can become stiff or slightly rusty in winter. Use a little vegetable oil to lubricate them.

Scissors, shears and clippers

Gardening equipment stored in a shed tends to stiffen up over the winter months when it may not be in use.

Apply a little vegetable oil and the tools will be easier to use. Apply to the joints with an old paintbrush.

INGREDIENTS

30nl/2 tbsp vegetable oil

1 feather

1 This is an old-fashioned trick for getting oil into a lock. Pour the oil into a saucer.

2 Dip the feather into the oil before inserting it in the lock.

Variations

Alternatively, dip the end of the key into the oil and then insert it into the lock. Drip oil on a stiff or slightly corroded padlock to loosen it. Once it is open, dip the open end in oil and open and shut the lock a few times to lubricate it.

Stacked glasses

If glasses that have been stacked get stuck together, free them with oil.

Pour a small amount of vegetable oil around the rim of the bottom glass. Gently pull the glasses apart – they should separate with ease.

Stiff screws

This is a good solution for old screws that are not badly corroded but just a little stiff.

Place a little oil in a saucer and use a small paintbrush to brush oil on to the screws. A hint of grape seed oil, which is very light, will go a long way but any vegetable oil will help.

Lubricating a sharpening stone

An inexpensive stone is brilliant for keeping kitchen knives sharp. Use vegetable oil to lubricate the stone.

Buy a double-sided sharpening stone, with one side slightly coarser than the other. Drop a little oil on to the fine sharpening side of the stone to finish off sharpening the knives.

Rings on your fingers

When a ring is rather tight and difficult to remove over the knuckle, a little oil may help.

Reduce any swelling as far as possible by holding under cold water and pat it dry. Trickle a little oil on the finger and the ring should slip over the knuckle. Repeat if necessary, taking care not to inflame the finger.

Door hinges

Use oil to loosen a stiff or squeaky hinge.

To avoid oil going everywhere, use a dropper or dip a cotton pad in oil and squeeze it out over the top of the hinge.

Loosening zips

If a zip becomes stuck, loosen it with oil.

Dip a cotton bud in olive oil and dab on to the teeth of the zip, before gently pulling it open.

Hinged furniture

Use oil to stop hinged seats squeaking.

Occasionally brush a little oil on to furniture that has metal mechanisms, for example folding chairs or swinging garden seats.

CLEANING AN OIL PAINTING

This is a good way of gently removing dust and dirt from an inexpensive painting that has been hanging in a room with an open fire.

4 Rub with a sponge moistened with a little tepid water before drying. Polish with a piece of silk cloth.

5 Finish by polishing the painting with a piece of flannel dampened with the boiled linseed oil.

INGREDIENTS
30ml/2 tbsp boiled linseed oil
1 potato

1 To freshen up an old oil painting, moisten a piece of cotton wool with a little boiled linseed oil and gently rub it over the surface of the painting.

2 If it still requires a more thorough clean, first cut the potato in half and dip the cut end into cold water.

3 Shake off excess water and rub lightly over the surface of the painting, then wipe with a damp sponge.

WARNING
These methods should only be used on inexpensive paintings. Do not attempt to clean valuable paintings yourself – these should always be taken to professional art restorers.

OIL AND PAINT

Oil is the medium used for mixing pigments in manufactured oil paints. Oils are also added by artists to dilute the concentrated paint from the tube. Depending on the type of oil added, the paint sets quickly or slowly. Oils commonly used include linseed, poppyseed, walnut and safflower.

OTHER USES FOR OILS IN THE HOME

Beyond the more obvious wood treatments and lubricating, oil can be put to use in other, more suprising ways, from keeping the rust off screws to removing paint from the skin.

Storing screws

This is an old-fashioned but practical way of storing screws, especially for items that are usually used outdoors rather than in clean paintwork in the house.

Some screws are galvanized but others tend to rust, particularly if they are stored outside, in a shed. Instead of leaving them in packets, put them in plastic containers and add a few drops of oil to each. Shake and cover. This will prevent them from rusting.

Shoe care

Traditionally, oils were used to preserve and protect shoe leather. Linseed oil was used for black shoes, castor oil for tan-coloured shoes and olive oil with a little jet black ink added for black patent shoes.

Rub new black shoes with a little olive oil on a cloth to preserve the finish and make cleaning easier. For a quick shoe polish, mix 2 parts olive oil to one part lemon juice and rub into leather shoes with a clean cloth.

Removing labels

Plastic and glass jars are handy to have around the house. Removing labels can be tricky, but soaking in oil will remove any residue.

Fill a small bowl with vegetable oil. Soak the jar(s) in the oil for a few hours, or overnight. The next day, the label will slide right off, taking any sticky glue residue with it. This method also works well for removing sticky price tags.

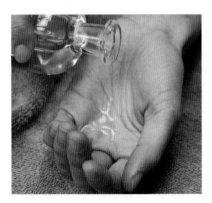

Removing paint

Use oil to clean the skin after painting.

Rub olive oil on to the skin and allow to soak into the skin for about 5 minutes, then rinse off with warm soapy water.

Treating cricket bats

Linseed oil is the traditional coating for the raw willow wood of cricket bats.

Lightly sand the surface of the bat then rub linseed oil into the wood with a clean cloth.

OILCLOTHS AND OILSKINS

Old-fashioned oilcloth was made by treating fabric with boiled linseed oil and allowing the surface to dry.

Oilcloths were the first wipe-clean protective surface covers used on kitchen tables, since they were waterproof and very resilient to damage. Old and tired oilcloth tablecloths can be revived by cleaning with a little boiled linseed oil.

Oilskins, which were traditionally worn by fishermen and sailors, were made in much the same way to produce heavy waterproof garments that were inflexible and rather brittle.

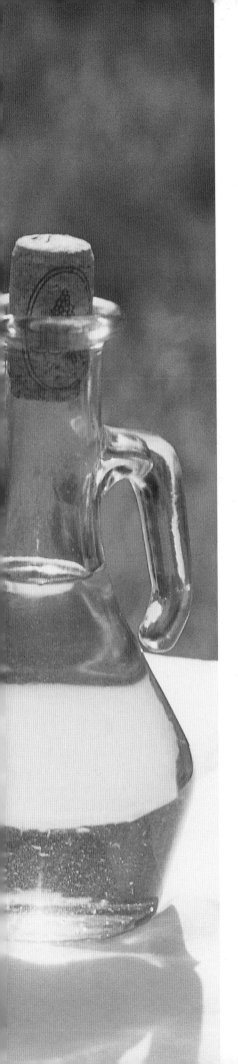

OILS IN THE KITCHEN

Vegetable oils have many roles to play around the house. They can be found in the bathroom cabinet, on the dressing table and in the garden shed, but they are most thoroughly at home in the kitchen. Oils have been used by cooks for many generations in different dishes around the world. They are an important part of a balanced diet and should be included in any store cupboard as a basic ingredient. Frying, marinating, basting, flavouring or simply dressing – this section will help you to explore the many culinary uses of oils.

Left: Vegetable oils can be used in food preparation just as they are, or can be easily flavoured with herbs and spices.

OILS AND DIET

Vegetable oils have many health benefits. They are high in vitamin E and a good source of the fats our bodies need. A variety of oils should be included as part of a balanced diet.

Although low-fat and even fat-free products are popular in today's health-conscious society, we all need to consume a small amount of fat to maintain a healthy and balanced diet. The fat in vegetable oils is a valuable source of energy, and also helps make food more palatable to eat.

Small quantities of polyunsaturated fats are essential for good health and are thought to help reduce the level of cholesterol in the blood. Oils that are a good source of polyunsaturated fats include safflower, corn, sunflower, soya, grape seed and cottonseed oils.

Monounsaturated fats are also though to have the beneficial effect of reducing the blood cholesterol level, and this could explain why in some Mediterranean countries there is such a low incidence of heart disease. Monounsaturated fats are

Above: Olive oil is an essential part of Mediterranean cuisine and a good source of monounsaturated fat, which is thought to play a role in reducing cholesterol levels.

found in nuts such as almonds and hazelnuts, oily fish and avocados. Oils which are a good source of monounsaturated fats include olive, rapeseed (canola), groundnut (peanut) and rice bran oil.

The Mediterranean diet
Olive oil has been used in cooking in Mediterranean countries for centuries. Crete has the highest consumption of olive oil per head in the world: it also has the lowest death rate from cardiovascular disease and the highest proportion of centenarians – a persuasive argument for the merits of the style of eating that is now commonly described as the 'Mediterranean diet'.

Because the Mediterranean region offers little pasture land for raising animals, but does have a lot of sun and sea, its people have traditionally lived on large quantities of ripe fruit and vegetables, herbs, seafood and bread, with relatively little meat and dairy produce.

The Nordic diet
Eating a diet based around the foods local to the Mediterranean region, including olive oil, has long been recommended as a healthy option. However, new research has now shown that the foods traditionally eaten in Scandinavian countries, Norway in particular, may also be among the healthiest.

NUT OILS AND ALLERGIES

Peanut allergies are among the most common food allergies, and the reactions can be severe.

People who suffer from peanut or other nut allergies should avoid using groundnut (peanut) and other nut oils.

The 'Nordic diet' is based around foods which are typically consumed in northern Europe, such as fresh fish and shellfish, leafy green vegetables (such as cabbage and kale) and native berries (such as blueberries and cloudberries). Unlike the Mediterranean countries that use large quantities of olive oil, the most commonly used cooking oil in Scandinavia is rapeseed (canola) oil. Rapeseed oil contains more omega-3 fatty acids than olive oil and is a very good source of vitamin E.

Obesity rates are among the lowest in Scandinavian countries when compared with the rest of Europe, a fact which can only add to the growing popularity of the Nordic diet among the health conscious.

Other health benefits of oil

Cold pressed vegetable oils, (as well as nuts and seeds) are important sources of vitamin E. Known as an important antioxidant, vitamin E plays many roles in ensuring heart and nervous system health, promoting healing and helping to prevent the skin from scarring. Sesame oil is rich in vitamin E and also contains magnesium, copper, calcium, iron and vitamin B6. Linseed oil is said to be an anti-inflammatory, and research is being carried out into the effects of linseed oil as a treatment for sufferers of rheumatoid arthritis. Grape seed oil is believed to lower cholesterol.

Taking small doses of olive oil has been recommended for centuries to aid digestion and reduce the effects of alcohol. Modern studies are still adding to an impressive list of the ways in which eating it regularly can improve your health.

Include olive oil in your diet and it may reduce gastric acidity, and help to protect against ulcers. It helps to prevent constipation, and may even reduce the risk of colon cancer. It stimulates bile secretion and reduces the risk of gallstones.

The antioxidants in extra virgin oil may help to reduce blood pressure. During pregnancy, oleic acid and vitamin E aid the development of the baby's bones, brain and nervous system. It relieves wear and tear on the brain and other organs, reducing the effects of ageing. It also speeds the healing of wounds.

Above: A Scandinavian favourite – marinated fish served with a mustard and dill sauce made with rapeseed oil. The Nordic diet is high in omega-3 fatty acids.

FISH OILS

Fish oils are promoted for their vitamin A and D, and omega-3 fatty acid contents. The fish do not make their own oils but they acquire them through their diet of marine life, especially algae. Currently fish oils are extracted from the waste products from fish and the remaining material is used for fishmeal.

There is much on-going research into ways of introducing omega-3 fatty acids into the human food chain without relying on fish. The natural diet of fish is obviously a source of key interest. Foods are already being supplemented with good fats but the aim for the future is to genetically modify oils as feed for animals, so that they yield meat or eggs that are a source of good fats. Fish oil capsules are often sold in health stores as a dietary supplement.

CULINARY USES OF OILS

Vegetable oils are a staple ingredient in any store cupboard. Oils have been used in the kitchen since ancient times in many different cuisines.

There are three main functions of oil in food preparation: as a cooking medium, to moisten dry foods and make them palatable, and to impart flavour.

Cooking in or with oils

Frying, grilling (broiling), roasting and baking are all methods that use cooking oil (or other fat). Oils used in cooking have to withstand high temperatures without breaking down, smoking and developing unpleasant flavours and unwanted trans fats.

Frying Cooking in or with oil on top of the hob is called frying. Deep-frying immerses the food in oil while shallow-frying cooks the food in a shallow layer of oil. Pan frying is a contemporary term for shallow-frying in minimal oil to prevent the food from sticking;

Above: Oil is drizzled over fish before it is covered and baked in the oven. The oil will impart moisture and flavour to the dish as it cooks.

Above: Stir-frying food in oil is a traditional Eastern cooking technique.

it was adopted instead of 'frying' when the latter became suggestive of unhealthy cooking. Stir-frying is cooking in oil while stirring and tossing the food constantly. Associated with Chinese, Japanese and South-east Asian cooking, stir-frying has acquired a reputation for low-fat cooking. In fact, stir-fried food is not necessarily low in fat but it depends on whether the classic techniques of cooking in stages and adding oil as needed are used, or whether food is simply cooked in one or two stages in the minimum of oil (the modern, Western style of stir-frying). Sautéing, the classic French equivalent of stir-frying, is cooking in oil over high heat while

turning, stirring and tossing the food constantly. For deep-frying, sautéing and stir-frying, the pan and oil have to reach a minimum temperature. Immersing food in oil that is not sufficiently hot makes it greasy.

Grilling (broiling) This form of cooking involves direct heat, either from above, or below (as with a barbecue). Oil is brushed over food before and during grilling to keep it moist and make it crisp.

Roasting This is a method of cooking in the oven, uncovered, without liquid but with fat, such as oil, to baste the food and keep it moist. Traditionally, roasting was done on a rack or a rotating spit, allowing

Above: Richly flavoured olive oil is often served as a dip for fresh bread.

the fat to drip off. Now the food is usually placed in a pan with the fat in the bottom.

Baking This method of oven cooking includes several variations. For example, when breads, cakes, pastries, soufflés and gratins or savoury dishes are baked, the mixture or ingredients are assembled in a tin (pan) or dish. Oil may be included as part of the basic mixture. Some foods are moistened with a little fat or oil before baking, for example fish or vegetables

may be moistened with butter or oil and cooked in a covered dish, or wrapped in foil, in the oven. Oil is also used to grease dishes or tins to prevent mixtures from sticking during cooking.

Moistening with oil

In addition to acting as a cooking medium, oil is used in several other ways to moisten food. The most basic example is serving oil as a dip for bread – of course, the purpose is to savour full-flavoured oil and good bread but moistening the bread also makes it more palatable.

In the broader sense, oil moistens food when used in cooking and when it is drizzled over as a dressing or used in sauces. Marinating is also used for moistening, tenderizing and flavouring food. Vinegar, wine or fruit juice may be used with oil for marinating, and herbs, spices or other flavouring ingredients are usually added. Marinating can take place over several hours or days in the refrigerator or for a short period at room temperature depending on the main ingredients and the results required.

Oil as a flavouring ingredient

Many oils have a distinctive flavour. There are many types of olive oil and some are used for their taste, particularly as a dressing for food, to finish a soup or as a dip for bread. Nut oils vary in strength but even the mild macadamia nut oil is quite distinctive. They are particularly useful in dressings and sauces, and they may also be used in sweet dishes, such as chilled desserts.

OIL AS A PRESERVATIVE

Immersing ingredients in oil can be a way of preserving them by excluding air.

However, simply covering foods with oil does not necessarily mean they will keep safely. Commercial processing involves sterilizing the contents to ensure that they are safe. The particular danger is from anaerobic bacteria that thrive in conditions that exclude air.

Botulism is a severe type of food poisoning resulting from eating food contaminated with the *Clostridium botulinum* bacteria; it can be fatal. The contaminated food may look edible.

Bottled foods that have not been properly sterilized and uncooked foods that are preserved in mixtures with low-acidity levels are vulnerable. The high levels of vinegar and sugar in chutneys and pickles together with the cooking process prevents spoilage.

Above: Add the finishing touch to simple salads with an oil dressing.

Above: Oils are used as a flavouring ingredient in many sauces and dips.

FRYING WITH OILS

From light and crispy deep-fried tempura to speedy stir-fries and sautéed vegetables, the primary way in which oil is used in the kitchen is for frying.

The main point to remember when using oil in cooking is that some types can withstand very high temperatures while others will burn easily, break down, lose their flavour and develop an unpleasant bitter taste.

Recognizing overheating
When oil heats it runs more easily, becoming less viscous and more like a water-based liquid. Tilt a pan when heating oil and notice that it soon runs more easily than when it was cold. When it gets very hot, the oil begins to shimmer slightly – this is the last stage of heating before the oil becomes too hot to use. The shimmering stage is used for some oils that can withstand high heat and for shallow frying some foods. When the oil forms a haze, that means that it has overheated and spoilt.

Checking oil temperature
There are different ways of checking the temperature of oil depending on the cooking method.

Deep-frying Using a sugar thermometer designed for checking high temperatures is the best way of checking the temperature of oil used for deep-frying. As a general rule, the oil should be heated to 180–190°C/350–375°F. Alternatively, use an electric deep-fat fryer. These have thermostats built in.

Cooking a small cube of day-old bread is another method of checking the temperature. When added to oil for deep-frying, the bread should brown in 30–60 seconds.

Shallow-frying or stir-frying When the amount of oil is small, tilt the pan to check the way it flows. When it begins to flow freely it is hot enough for cooking.

Double check by adding a small piece of food first: the food should sizzle immediately but not so harshly that it will burn. Another old-fashioned but successful method is to add a drip of water – just a drip and no more. The fat should spit and sizzle. Adding any more than a drip can be dangerous as the fat will sizzle and spit severely.

DEEP-FRY ALTERNATIVES

Deep-frying is not a very popular cooking method nowadays, and many kitchens do not have a pan suitable for deep-frying. Although a large saucepan can be used, many cooks compromise by frying in about 2.5cm/1in of oil in a sauté pan or wok. The food may not be entirely submerged and therefore it is turned halfway through cooking, but it is effectively deep-fried. Breadcrumb coatings and some batters are suitable for this method. Very light, soft or runny batters may not work on large pieces of food.

SMOKING POINT
When heating oil for cooking, smoking point is the ultimate overheating stage. When this stage is reached, an acrid smell and fine but dark and distinct smoke will be produced. Allowing the oil to heat to this stage not only makes it completely unusable but it is also dangerous as it will easily ignite. Apart from poor flavour and quality, when fats are altered at molecular level this releases free radicals and produces trans fatty acids which should be avoided as far as possible in the diet.

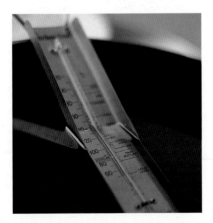

Above: A sugar thermometer can be used to test oil used for deep-frying.

Above: If a cube of bread browns within 60 seconds, the oil is ready to use.

Coating before cooking

The purpose of coating food is to protect the surface of delicate foods from the high temperature of oil to prevent excess drying, disintegration or over cooking. The type of coating depends on the food and frying technique.

Dusting with flour This is useful for shallow frying foods that will not disintegrate in the minimum oil. The oil may form the basis for a sauce and some of the flour from the food may thicken the sauce. Meat, poultry or fish may be floured before frying in a little oil.

Breadcrumbs and batter provide more protection. Egg and breadcrumbs can be used to coat small or large pieces of food, for shallow frying or deep-frying. Batter is not suitable for shallow-frying in the minimum of oil as it will run off but it is used for protecting foods for deep-frying.

Coating with breadcrumbs This is usually referred to as an egg and bread coating. Coating the food with egg enables the breadcrumbs to stick in the first place, then the egg sets quickly and the breadcrumbs form a crisp coating. So that the egg does not slip off, the food is first dusted with flour. Chilling the coated food helps to set the egg and breadcrumb mixture and keep it in place during cooking.

Coating with batter There are several types of batter, some very light and fine, others more robust. The type depends on the food and recipe. The simplest batter is a mixture of self-raising (self-rising) or plain (all-purpose) flour and water, beaten until smooth. The thicker the mixture, the thicker the coating. Thick plain batter is generally unpleasant and a basic batter should be thin. Milk may be used instead of water, as part or all of the amount, although milk tends to make the batter heavy.

Above: Japanese tempura is coated in a very light batter. This lightness is achieved by minimal mixing. The batter protects the food from the very hot oil.

Above: A light coating of flour is often used for food that is shallow fried.

Above: Breadcrumbs will form a crisp coating on food when it is fried.

Eggs may be added, either whole or separated. When separated, the yolks are beaten in first with a little water to make a thick batter, then the whites are whisked until stiff and folded in. This makes a very light batter that rises and becomes thin and crisp during cooking – even if the layer is thicker, because the mixture rises it is far lighter in texture. Fizzy beer is another classic ingredient for making a light batter.

Some batters are prepared by minimum mixing, typically Japanese tempura batter. This very light batter is used to coat pieces of seafood, chopped vegetables and other ingredients, providing a very thin, crisp and 'open' batter. The mixing is so minimal that having tiny pockets of flour is expected – these should not be beaten out as this will give a heavier result.

Perfect deep-frying

Oil used for deep-frying should be able to withstand high temperatures. The best choices are groundnut (peanut), sunflower and blended vegetable oil intended for frying. Olive oil is not used for deep-frying (although there are some exceptions in esoteric recipes).

In this method of frying, the aim is to produce a crisp result that is dry, with the minimum retention of oil at the end of cooking. The oil does not usually flavour the food, but there are exceptions, for example when cooking in corn oil.

A wide variety of foods can be deep-fried as long as it cooks quickly and is tender. The majority of foods need to be protected by an outer coating before deep-frying to prevent the surface from drying out, to retain moisture and to prevent mixtures from disintegrating.

Successful shallow-frying

When using oil for shallow-frying, it is important to differentiate between cooking in oil simply for the 'fried' result and cooking in a particular oil for its flavour.

Shallow-frying in a small amount of olive oil or a blend of sunflower and sesame oil will contribute to the flavour of the dish. Shallow-frying in blended vegetable oil, grapeseed oil or refined groundnut (peanut) oil will produce a 'fried' flavour but without any characteristics of the oil.

Frying for texture When shallow-frying in bland oil, slightly more oil may be used (a thin coating all over the bottom of the pan) and the oil should be well heated before the food is added. The technique is the same as for deep-frying, except that the food has to be turned halfway through cooking. For this type of frying a steady temperature is maintained.

Frying for flavour When the oil is used as the base for a sauce or dressing to serve with the food, the type and amount is important; maintaining a steady cooking temperature may also be vital to cooking other items as well as the main ingredient. For example, fish may be fried in olive oil, then tomatoes, olives and spring onions may be fried in the same oil to be served with the fish.

Above: A small amount of vegetable, groundnut or grapeseed oil is used when shallow-frying food for texture. The oil should just coat the bottom of the pan.

TIPS FOR DEEP-FRYING WITH OIL

A deep pan should be used for frying a significant batch of food or large pieces. Small pieces or a few small items can be cooked in a 'puddle' of oil in the bottom of a wok or small pan but this is not safe for larger quantities. The pan should be one-third to half full of oil before heating and no more. When food is added the level will rise and the hot oil will bubble and froth up. If is boils over the edge of the pan it will easily catch fire.

When the food is added to the oil, the temperature drops. If too large a batch of food is added the oil will not reheat quickly and the food may become soggy and oily. Add small batches for quick, clean cooking.

Turn the food, if necessary, for even cooking. Some foods float and the top may not cook as quickly as the underside.

Always drain food thoroughly. A draining basket in a deep-frying pan allows batches of small items to be lowered into the hot oil and removed all at once. Alternatively, a draining spoon can be used. Let the oil drip off, then place the food on double-thick paper towels to absorb excess oil.

When cooking in several batches, always remove debris from the oil before adding fresh food as the small pieces of food will burn.

Reheat the oil between batches, taking care that it doesn't overheat.

Do not reuse oil more than once or twice – depending on the amount of food cooked, the type, temperature and number of batches. Strongly flavoured foods will taint the oil.

The cooking temperature may be far lower in this type of dish and the overall method more gentle to retain the flavour of the oil that will be scraped out of the pan with the juices and served as an accompaniment.

Slow shallow-frying When cooking thicker food items in shallow oil, it is a good idea to start at a higher temperature and turn the food to brown both sides, then reduce the heat and cook more slowly to allow time for the food to cook through. When using this technique, the flavour of the oil will be imparted to the food and the juices from the food will mix with the oil. The type and amount of oil is important, for example, a thin layer of olive oil may be used or a mixture of oil and butter. The pan juices may be seasoned and sharpened with lemon juice or balsamic (or other) vinegar and served with the food.

Speedy shallow-frying When shallow frying ingredients that cook quickly, preheating the pan brings the oil up to temperature quickly. The disadvantage is that this method is fierce: the oil heats rapidly when added to a very hot pan and

Above: Use a flat-bottomed sauté pan for ingredients that do not take long to cook, such as mushrooms.

it can overheat very quickly. This method is not suitable for non-stick coated pans that should not be heated empty.

Classic sautéing

A sauté pan has a flat bottom and slightly deeper sides than the average frying pan. This allows food to be tossed, shaken and turned. This method

Above: Olive oil is not generally suitable for deep-frying, but is used to impart flavour to shallow fried dishes.

is good for firm but tender ingredients that cook quickly, for example medallions (small, fairly thin round slices) of chicken, pork or lamb; boiled potatoes; or mushrooms.

The ingredients should be cut into even-sized pieces that cook quickly. Refined groundnut (peanut) oil or grape seed oil can be heated to a high temperature and they can be combined with butter. The food should be cooked over high heat and turned and tossed regularly until evenly browned.

Quick and healthy stir-frying

Unlike sautéing, stir-frying usually involves adding small amounts of several different types of foods in stages. Foods that take longest to cook are cooked first, then pushed aside to make room for additional ingredients. All the ingredients have to be cut up evenly into pieces that cook quickly before beginning stir-frying. The pan has to be big enough to hold all the food or the ingredients that are cooked first have to be removed and then replaced at a later stage.

Above: Groundnut oil is popular for stir-frying. Ingredients should all be cut to the same size so that they all cook at the same rate. A little sesame oil can be added for flavour.

CULINARY TRICKS WITH OILS

Most cooks will be used to using oil in their cooking, but it is also helpful for other purposes, from seasoning a wok to greasing tins and as a preserving agent.

Greasing tins (pans)

Use a little mild-flavoured vegetable oil such as sunflower oil to grease cake tins, patty tins (muffin pans) and baking trays.

Use a pastry brush or pour a little of the oil on to a paper towel and wipe around the tin. This will stop cakes or muffins sticking to the tins.

Making freezer preserves

These can be kept in the freezer for up to 3 months, ready for adding to a salad, for topping a pizza or enriching a casserole.

Drizzle vegetables such as tomatoes, (bell) peppers, chillies or mushrooms with olive oil, cook slowly until concentrated in flavour. Allow to cool, place in a suitable container then cover with oil. Freeze in small portions.

Seasoning and cleaning a wok

Carbon steel woks are sold with a coating to protect them from rust. Seasoning will remove this and make the wok non-stick.

1 Wash the wok thoroughly in warm, soapy water to remove any coating. Rinse well, shake off excess water, then place over a low heat to dry.

2 Add a little oil (not olive oil) and, using kitchen paper, wipe the pan to coat it evenly. Take care not to burn yourself. Heat gently for 10 minutes, then wipe off the oil with clean kitchen paper. Don't be alarmed when it blackens – this is natural.

3 Repeat the process for as long as it takes for the paper to come away clean, by which time the wok itself will have darkened. The more it is used, the better the wok's natural non-stick coating will become and the easier it will be to clean.

4 A properly seasoned wok should never be washed with soap. After use, remove any food that sticks to the surface, then wash in hot water. Dry thoroughly by placing the wok over a low heat for a few minutes. Leave to cool, then rub a little oil into the surface.

Oiling a chopping board

Wooden chopping boards, or 'butcher's blocks' need oiling to stop them cracking.

Place 30ml/2 tbsp walnut oil in a small dish and warm in the microwave. Using a clean cloth, liberally apply the oil to the board, rubbing in the direction of the grain. Allow the oil to soak in for 2 minutes, then apply a second coat in the same way. After use, the board should be washed in hot soapy water and dried straight away. If anyone who will use the chopping board has a nut allergy, edible mineral oil (sold as butcher's block oil) should be used instead of walnut oil.

Maintaining a barbecue

Use oil on the barbecue before and after cooking to keep it in top condition.

Before using your barbecue, wipe the grill with a little vegetable oil on a pastry brush. This will prevent food from sticking to the grill. To clean the hot plate of a barbecue, brush with vegetable oil and heat up the plate. The hot oil will make it easier to scrape off any hardened burnt food residue with a spatula. Once it is clean, allow the plate to cool, then brush lightly with oil to prevent rust from forming.

Making super-light cakes

Add a small proportion of sunflower oil, increasing the eggs and flour accordingly.

When making plain creamed cakes, for example, place 115g/4oz butter and 175g/6oz /^{2}/3 cup caster (superfine) sugar in a bowl, then trickle in 45 ml/ 3 tbsp sunflower oil. Cream the mixture as usual, adding 5–10 ml/1–2 tsp vanilla extract, then add 3 eggs with a little flour from 200g/7oz/1^3/4 cups self-raising (self-rising) flour. Fold in the flour and finish as usual – the result is a delicious light sponge cake.

Making crispy baked potatoes

Brush olive oil or rapeseed (canola) oil on to baking potatoes for extra-crispy skin.

Wash and dry your potatoes thoroughly, then brush with oil and add a generous sprinkling of sea salt. Place on a baking tray and cook in the middle of a hot oven at 220°C/425°F/Gas 7 for 1–1^1/2 hours.

Making Mediterranean mash

Transform your mashed potatoes with a little olive oil and Parmesan cheese.

To make a Mediterranean version of classic mashed potatoes, beat in 15ml/ 1 tbsp olive oil, and season with salt and black pepper. Serve sprinkled with finely grated Parmesan cheese.

Making bread

Making your own bread is very satisfying. Use oiled clear film to help it rise.

Once you have made your dough, always cover it with oiled clear film (plastic wrap) to rise. This will prevent the dough from forming a crust. Coating the clear film with oil will stop the dough from sticking to it.

FLAVOURING OILS

Good quality oil can be flavoured with herbs, spices and aromatics to make rich-tasting oils that are perfect for drizzling, making dressings and cooking.

Garlic oil

A first choice herb oil ingredient, garlic is thought to ward off infections. Flavouring oil with garlic is a wonderful way to preserve the tastes of summer, as it can be stored in a cool, dry place for 3–6 months.

INGREDIENTS

5–6 large whole cloves of garlic
600ml/1 pint/2$^{1}/_{2}$ cups oil

1 First carefully peel each of the whole garlic cloves.

2 Push the cloves into clean, dry bottles. If the cloves are too large for the neck of the bottle, cut them in half lengthways.

3 Fill the bottles to the top with the oil, and cork. Leave for 2 weeks to infuse (steep). Check the flavour and strain the oil through a muslin- (cheesecloth-) lined sieve (strainer).

4 Pour into clean bottles and keep refrigerated for up to 2 months.

Cayenne and garlic oil

This is a richly flavoured oil with a kick.

Place 10–15ml/2–3 tsp cayenne pepper and 4 crushed garlic cloves into a clean, dry bottle and pour in 300ml/$^{1}/_{2}$ pint/1$^{1}/_{4}$ cups oil. Leave to infuse (steep) for 2 weeks, then strain and bottle. Keep refrigerated and use within 2 months.

WHICH OILS TO USE?

When flavouring your own oils, use a base oil that is not too strongly flavoured, such as groundnut (peanut), sunflower, safflower or a light olive oil. Avoid using cheap, blended vegetable oils. You should always store home-flavoured oils in the refrigerator.

Chilli and tomato oil

Heating oil with chillies intensifies the rich flavour. This tastes great sprinkled over pasta dishes.

INGREDIENTS
150ml/¹/4 pint/²/3 cup oil
10ml/2 tsp tomato purée (paste)
15ml/1 tbsp dried red chilli flakes

1 Heat the oil in a large pan. When it is very hot, but not smoking, stir in the tomato purée followed by the chilli flakes.

2 Leave the flavoured oil to cool completely in the pan, then pour it into an airtight jar and store in the refrigerator for up to 2 months.

Dried chilli oil

Leave the chillies in the bottle for a pleasant decorative effect.

Add several dried chillies to a bottle of oil and leave to infuse (steep) for about 2 weeks before using. If the flavour is not sufficiently pronounced, leave for another week. Keep refrigerated for up to 2 months.

Chilli spice oil

Mixed spices enrich this chilli oil.

Add 1 peeled and halved garlic clove, 3 dried red chillies, 5ml/1 tsp coriander seeds, 5ml/ 1 tsp allspice berries, 6 black peppercorns, 4 juniper berries and 2 bay leaves to a bottle of oil. Seal tightly and leave in a cool, dark place for 2 weeks. If the flavour is not sufficiently pronounced, leave the oil to infuse (steep) for another week before straining. Keep refrigerated and use within 2 months.

Basil oil

This has a delicious Mediterranean flavour. The flavour of basil is notoriously difficult to preserve when the herb is dried or frozen, but a well-made basil oil retains all the subtle flavour of the fresh herb. If you wish, use oil that has already been infused with garlic.

INGREDIENTS

about 15g/^{1}/$_2$oz/^{1}/$_2$ cup basil leaves

450ml/^{3}/$_4$ pint/scant 2 cups oil

1 Place the basil leaves in a mortar and pestle and begin to bruise the leaves lightly.

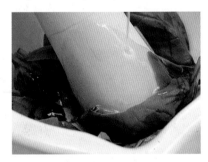

2 Gradually drizzle in about 30ml/ 2 tbsp of the oil. Gently combine the oil with the basil.

3 Pour the oil and basil mixture into a clean, dry glass bottle and top up with the rest of the oil. Cover and store in a cool place for 2–3 weeks.

4 Pour the infused basil oil through a muslin- (cheesecloth-) lined sieve (strainer). Leave the oil to drip through the muslin without squeezing the leaves. Pour the strained oil into a clean glass bottle, seal and keep chilled for 2–3 weeks.

Mixed herb oil

Follow this method to flavour oil with different herbs and spices. Parsley, sage and thyme are a good combination, but marjoram, rosemary, bay and sage are also good used together, or singly.

Pour 600ml/1 pint/2^1/$_2$ cups oil into a jar and 125g/4^1/$_4$oz mixed chopped fresh herbs, such as parsley, sage and thyme. Cover and allow to stand at room temperature for about a week, no longer. Shake occasionally during that time. Strain off the oil into a bottle and discard the used herbs. Seal the jar carefully. Store in the refrigerator for up to 6 months.

Lemon oil

Drizzle this subtle fruity oil over pasta dishes. It is good with shellfish.

Finely pare the rind from 1 lemon, place on kitchen paper, and leave to dry for 1 day. Add the dried rind to a bottle of oil and leave to infuse (steep) for up to 3 days. Strain the oil into a clean bottle and discard the rind. Keep refrigerated and use within 2 months.

Spring onion (scallion) oil

The subtle flavour of this spring onion oil make it a great choice for a dressing.

Pour the 250ml/8fl oz/1 cup oil into a pan and heat gently. Stir in 8 finely sliced spring onions (scallions) and remove from the heat. Leave to infuse (steep) until completely cool, then pour the oil into a clean jar or bottle and seal tightly. Store in the refrigerator until ready to use, for up to 2 months.

HERB OILS

- Vegetable oils are widely recognized as being a healthier addition to the diet than butter and other saturated animal fats. Flavoured with herbs, they add a new dimension to cooking.

- As well as tasting delicious, flavoured oils take on the medicinal properties of the herbs used, and so are important constituents of many healing remedies and natural products.

- Oils containing fresh herbs and spices can grow the harmful moulds that can cause botulism. The particular risk is from anaerobic bacteria which thrive when air is excluded. To protect against this, it is recommended that the herbs and spices are removed once their flavour has passed to the oil.

- Adding fresh chillies to a herb oil produces a fiery condiment: try dribbling a tiny amount on to pasta dishes for extra flavour.

Marjoram flower oil

Use any flowers that you have an abundance of to make a fragrant flavoured oil. Thyme, rosemary, lavender, mint and basil are all great alternatives to marjoram flowers. Flower oil makes a perfect summer salad dressing.

INGREDIENTS

30–40 marjoram flower clusters, clean dry and free of insects

450ml/3/4 pint/scant 2 cups oil

1 Fill a large, clean, dry jam jar with the flower clusters (do not worry about removing any small leaves).

2 Pour oil into the jar, covering the flowers, making sure that they are all submerged.

3 Cover with a lid and leave in a warm place for 2 weeks, shaking the jar occasionally.

4 Line a small sieve (strainer) with clean muslin (cheesecloth) or a coffee filter bag and position over a jug (pitcher).

5 Carefully strain the oil into the jug, then pour into a clean attractive bottle. Seal and store in the refrigerator for 3–6 months.

OILS IN MARINADES

These strong-tasting mixes are perfect for adding flavour to meat, poultry, fish and vegetables. Most ingredients should be left to marinate for at least 30 minutes.

Moroccan harissa marinade

Coat fish or shellfish in this fiery marinade to create a dish that will transport you to the North African coastline.

In a small bowl, mix together 30ml/ 2 tbsp argan oil, 5ml/1 tsp harissa, 5ml/ 1 tsp clear honey and season with a pinch of salt.

Red wine and bay marinade

Marinades containing red wine are particularly good for tenderizing tougher cuts of meat such as stewing steak.

Whisk together 150ml/$^{1}/_{4}$ pint/$^{2}/_{3}$ cup red wine, 1 chopped garlic clove, 2 torn fresh bay leaves and 45ml/3 tbsp olive oil. Season with black pepper.

Sweet soy marinade

This can be used to marinade sirloin or fillet steak. It will give it a sweet-sour taste and an oriental feel.

Combine 75ml/5 tbsp dark soy sauce with 30ml/2 tbsp sesame oil with 2 crushed garlic cloves, 15ml/1 tbsp honey and 15ml/1tbsp sesame seeds.

Ginger and soy marinade

This Asian-style marinade is perfect for chicken that is going to be stir-fried.

Peel and grate a 2.5cm/1in piece of fresh root ginger and peel and finely chop a large garlic clove. Whisk together 60ml/4 tbsp olive oil with 75ml/5 tbsp dark soy sauce. Season and stir in the ginger and garlic.

Lemon grass and lime marinade

This light and zesty marinade is great with fish and chicken.

Finely chop 1 lemon grass stalk. In a small bowl, whisk together the grated rind and juice of 1 lime with 75ml/5 tbsp groundnut (peanut) oil, salt and black pepper and the lemon grass.

Rosemary and garlic marinade

This herby marinade is ideal for robust fish, lamb and chicken.

Roughly chop the leaves from 3 fresh rosemary sprigs. Finely chop 2 garlic cloves and whisk together with the rosemary, 75ml/5 tbsp rosemary herb oil and the juice of 1 large lemon.

OILS IN DRESSINGS

Oil is the classic dressing ingredient. These dressings are delicious drizzled over salads but are also tasty served with cooked vegetables and simply cooked fish, meat and poultry.

Walnut dressing

Spoon this dressing over new potatoes and garnish with snipped chives and toasted chopped walnuts.

Combine 30ml/2 tbsp walnut oil with 120ml/4fl oz/1/2 cup low-fat fromage frais or yogurt and add 15ml/1 tbsp chopped fresh flat leaf parsley. Season to taste.

Lemon herb dressing

This quick and easy dressing makes an excellent accompaniment to fish and vegetables.

In a small bowl, whisk together 45ml/ 3 tbsp mixed herb oil with the juice of 1 lemon. Stir in a pinch of dried oregano and season to taste.

Orange and tarragon dressing

Serve this fresh, tangy dressing with salads and grilled (broiled) fish. It will add a light fruity taste.

Whisk together the rind and juice of 1 orange with 45ml/3 tbsp olive oil and 15ml/1 tbsp chopped fresh tarragon. Season with salt and plenty of ground black pepper to taste.

Blue cheese and walnut dressing

Serve this rich dressing with a refreshing sliced pear and watercress salad.

Crumble and then mash 25g/1 oz blue cheese into 30ml/2 tbsp walnut oil. Whisk in 15ml/1 tbsp lemon juice to create a thickish mixture. Season to taste with salt and pepper.

Coconut chilli dressing

This Thai-style dressing is scented with creamy coconut and hot chilli.

Mix 15ml/1 tbsp creamed coconut (coconut cream), 45ml/3 tbsp boiling water, 60ml/4 tbsp groundnut (peanut) oil, rind and juice of 1 lime, 1 chopped red chilli, 5ml/1 tsp sugar and 45ml/3 tbsp chopped fresh coriander (cilantro).

Coriander dressing

This simple dressing made with sesame oil has a pleasing bite.

Mix 120ml/4fl oz/1/2 cup lemon juice, 30ml/2 tbsp wholegrain mustard, 250ml/8fl oz/1 cup olive oil, 75ml/5 tbsp sesame oil and 5ml/1 tsp crushed coriander seeds together in a bowl.

OILS IN SAUCES

In these sauce recipes, oil is infused with other stronger flavourings and ingredients. Adding nut oils to sauces containing fresh nuts will really bring out their flavour.

Olive oil, tomato and herb sauce

This Mediterranean sauce is enriched with olive oil. Serve with fresh bread.

INGREDIENTS

Makes approx 450ml/³/4 pint/scant 2 cups

15ml/1 tbsp finely chopped shallot

2 garlic cloves, finely chopped

120ml/4fl oz/¹/2 cup olive oil

about 15ml/1 tbsp lemon juice

225g/8oz tomatoes, peeled, seeded and diced

caster (superfine) sugar

15ml/1 tbsp chopped fresh chervil

15ml/1 tbsp snipped fresh chives

30ml/2 tbsp torn fresh basil leaves

salt and ground black pepper

1 Place the shallot, garlic and oil in a pan over a low heat and allow to infuse (steep) for 2 minutes. Whisk in 30ml/2 tbsp cold water and 10ml/2 tsp lemon juice.

2 Remove from the heat and stir in the tomatoes. Add a pinch of salt, pepper and caster sugar, then whisk in the chervil and chives. Stand for 10 minutes. Reheat until just warm, stir in the basil, and serve.

Energy 773kcal/3186kJ; **Protein** 2.7g; **Carbohydrate** 9g, of which sugars 8.5g; **Fat** 81g, of which saturates 11.4g; **Cholesterol** 0mg; **Calcium** 80mg; **Fibre** 4g; **Sodium** 31mg.

Peanut sauce

The exotic flavour of this peanut sauce perfectly complements Thai food.

INGREDIENTS

Makes approx 300ml/¹/2 pint/1¹/4 cups

30ml/2 tbsp groundnut (peanut) oil

75g/3oz/³/4 cup unsalted peanuts, blanched

2 shallots, chopped

2 garlic cloves, chopped

15ml/1 tbsp chopped fresh root ginger

1–2 green chillies, seeded and thinly sliced

5ml/1 tsp ground coriander

1 lemon grass stalk, tender base only, chopped

5–10ml/1–2 tsp light muscovado (brown) sugar

15ml/1 tbsp dark soy sauce

105–120ml/3–4 fl oz/scant ¹/2 cup canned coconut milk

15–30ml/1–2 tbsp Thai fish sauce (nam pla)

15–30ml/1–2 tbsp tamarind purée (paste)

lime juice

salt and ground black pepper

1 Heat the oil in a small pan and fry the peanuts, stirring frequently, until lightly browned. Remove the nuts and drain on kitchen paper. Set aside to cool.

2 Add the shallots, garlic, ginger, most of the sliced chillies and the ground coriander to the pan and cook over a low heat, stirring, for 5 minutes, until the shallots are softened but not browned.

3 Transfer the spice mixture to a food processor or blender and add the peanuts, lemon grass, 5ml/1 tsp of the sugar, the soy sauce and 105ml/3fl oz of coconut milk and the fish sauce. Blend to a smooth sauce. Add more fish sauce, tamarind purée, seasoning, lime juice and/or more sugar to taste. Serve.

Energy 339kcal/1399kJ; **Protein** 4.8g; **Carbohydrate** 5.1g, of which sugars 2.8g; **Fat** 33.4g, of which saturates 3.5g; **Cholesterol** 0mg; **Calcium** 34mg; **Fibre** 1.2g; **Sodium** 32mg.

Chilli sauce

This hot and spicy sauce is made with groundnut oil – serve with Thai food.

INGREDIENTS

Makes approx 475ml/16fl oz/2 cups

10 fresh red chillies

4 garlic cloves

15ml/1 tbsp Thai fish sauce (nam pla)

15ml/1 tbsp grated palm sugar (jaggery) or soft brown sugar

30ml/2 tbsp lime juice

5ml/1 tsp salt

120ml/4fl oz water

45ml/3 tbsp groundnut (peanut) oil

1 Seed and finely chop the red chillies, and peel and finely chop the garlic cloves, then place in a small pan.

2 Add the rest of the ingredients to the pan and slowly bring to the boil.

3 Reduce the heat and simmer the mixture gently for about 15 minutes.

4 Transfer to a food processor or blender and blend until smooth.

5 Allow to cool, then pour the chilli sauce into a small airtight jar or bottle. The sauce can be stored in the refrigerator for up to 1 week.

Energy 425kcal/1760kJ; **Protein** 8.8g; **Carbohydrate** 21.6g, of which sugars 17.4g; **Fat** 34.3g, of which saturates 4g; **Cholesterol** 0mg; **Calcium** 75mg; **Fibre** 0.8g; **Sodium** 2839mg.

Walnut and garlic sauce

The addition of walnut oil to this sauce gives it a really rich nutty taste.

INGREDIENTS

Makes approx 475ml/16fl oz/2 cups

2 x 1cm/^{1}/$_2$in slices good white bread, crusts removed

60ml/4 tbsp milk

150g/5oz/1^1/$_4$ cups shelled walnuts

4 garlic cloves, peeled and chopped

120ml/4fl oz/^{1}/$_2$ cup olive oil

15–30ml/1–2 tbsp walnut oil

juice of 1 lemon

salt and ground black pepper

walnut oil for drizzling

1 Soak the slices of white bread in the milk for about 5 minutes, then process with the walnuts and chopped garlic in a food processor or blender, to make a rough paste.

2 Gradually add the olive oil to the paste with the motor still running, until the mixture forms a smooth thick sauce. Blend in the walnut oil.

3 Scoop the sauce into a bowl and squeeze in lemon juice to taste, season with salt and pepper and beat well. Transfer to a serving bowl, and drizzle over a little more walnut oil.

Energy 1906kcal/7870kJ; **Protein** 28.6g; **Carbohydrate** 34.6g, of which sugars 8.3g; **Fat** 184.7g, of which saturates 20.4g; **Cholesterol** 4mg; **Calcium** 272mg; **Fibre** 6.1g; **Sodium** 324mg.

Perfect mayonnaise

Making great mayonnaise is about slowly incorporating oil with egg yolk.

INGREDIENTS

Makes approx 250ml/8fl oz/1 cups

1 fresh egg yolk

5ml/1tsp French mustard

15ml/1 tbsp lemon juice or white wine vinegar

200ml/7fl oz/scant 1 cup oil

salt and ground black pepper

1 Whisk the egg yolk in a mixing bowl with the seasoning, the French mustard and the lemon juice or vinegar.

2 Pour the oil into a jug (pitcher): olive oil makes mayonnaise with a full flavour; for a lighter result, combine sunflower or grape seed and olive oil.

3 Trickle in a little oil and whisk until combined. Continue whisking while adding oil in a slow trickle, until the mixture is pale and starting to thicken.

4 As the mixture thickens, the oil can be added slightly more quickly – in a steady trickle. Keep whisking until you have a smooth, glossy mayonnaise.

5 The mayonnaise can be stored in the refrigerator in an airtight jar for 1 week.

Energy 958kcal/3940kJ; **Protein** 3.3g; **Carbohydrate** 0,5g, of which sugars 0.4g; **Fat** 104.8g, of which saturates 13.1g; **Cholesterol** 202mg; **Calcium** 27mg; **Fibre** 0g; **Sodium** 157mg.

OILS IN PURÉES AND PASTES

These purées and pastes can be served as an accompaniment to bread, or used as a starting point for other dishes, such as spicy curries or tasty pasta dishes.

Aubergine and yogurt purée

This rich and creamy purée is delicious served with fresh white bread.

INGREDIENTS

Makes approx 500ml/17fl oz/generous 2 cups
2 large aubergines (eggplants)
30ml/2 tbsp olive oil, plus extra for drizzling
juice of 1 lemon
2–3 garlic cloves, crushed
225g/8oz/1 cup natural (plain) yogurt
salt and ground black pepper

1 Grill (broil) the aubergines until the skin is charred and the flesh feels soft. Place in a plastic bag for a few minutes. Hold each aubergine by the stalk under cold running water and peel off the skin until you are left with just the flesh. Squeeze the flesh to get rid of excess water and chop to a pulp, discarding the stalks.

2 Put in a bowl with 30ml/2 tbsp oil, the lemon juice and garlic. Beat well to mix, then beat in the yogurt and season. Transfer to a bowl, drizzle with olive oil and serve immediately.

Energy 103kcal/431kJ; **Protein** 4.4g; **Carbohydrate** 7.7g, of which sugars 6.4g; **Fat** 6.5g, of which saturates 1.2g; **Cholesterol** 1mg; **Calcium** 118mg; **Fibre** 2.3g; **Sodium** 49mg.

Muhammara

Serve this nutty, spicy Middle Eastern purée with flatbreads.

INGREDIENTS

Makes approx 350ml/12fl oz/1½ cups
175g/6oz/1 cup broken shelled walnuts
5ml/1 tsp cumin seeds, dry-roasted and ground
1–2 fresh red chillies, seeded and finely chopped
1–2 garlic cloves
1 slice of day-old bread, sprinkled with water
   and left for a few minutes, then squeezed dry
15–30ml/1–2 tbsp tomato purée (paste)
5–10ml/1–2 tsp sugar
juice of 1 lemon
120ml/4fl oz/½ cup sunflower oil

1 Using a mortar and pestle, pound the walnuts with the cumin seeds, red chilli and garlic.

2 Add the soaked bread and pound to a paste, then beat in the tomato purée, sugar and lemon juice.

3 Drizzle in the oil, beating until the paste is thick. Season, and serve.

Energy 339kcal/1399kJ; **Protein** 4.8g; **Carbohydrate** 5.1g, of which sugars 2.8g; **Fat** 33.4g, of which saturates 3.5g; **Cholesterol** 0mg; **Calcium** 34mg; **Fibre** 1.2g; **Sodium** 32mg.

Curry paste

Cook spices in oil and store in the refrigerator for convenience.

INGREDIENTS

Makes approx 600ml/1 pint/2½ cups
50g/2oz/½ cup coriander seeds
60ml/4 tbsp cumin seeds
30ml/2 tbsp fennel seeds
30ml/2 tbsp fenugreek seeds
4 dried red chillies
5 curry leaves
15ml/1 tbsp chilli powder
15ml/1 tbsp ground turmeric
150ml/¼ pint/⅔ cup wine vinegar
250ml/8fl oz/1 cup sunflower or corn oil

1 Grind the whole spices to a powder. Transfer to a bowl and mix in the remaining ground spices. Add the vinegar and 75ml/5 tbsp water and stir to a paste.

2 Heat the oil and stir-fry the paste for 10 minutes or until the water is absorbed. When the oil rises to the surface it is cooked. Cool, spoon into airtight jars and store for up to 4 weeks in the refrigerator.

Energy 1949kcal/8040kJ; **Protein** 19.2g; **Carbohydrate** 45.4g, of which sugars 0g; **Fat** 191.7g, of which saturates 20.7g; **Cholesterol** 0mg; **Calcium** 234mg; **Fibre** 0g; **Sodium** 44mg.

Thai green curry paste

This fragrant spicy mix makes a delicious Thai curry.

INGREDIENTS

Makes approx 475ml/6fl oz/2 cups
12 fresh green chillies, seeded and chopped
15ml/1 tbsp finely grated garlic
10ml/2 tsp finely grated fresh root ginger
30ml/2 tbsp chopped lemon grass
4 kaffir lime leaves, finely snipped
4 red shallots, chopped
15ml/1 tbsp coriander seeds, roasted
50g/2oz coriander (cilantro) leaves, stalks
   and roots, roughly chopped
5ml/1 tsp ground black pepper
rind of 1 lime, finely grated
90ml/6 tbsp sunflower oil

1 Place all the ingredients in a food processor or blender.

2 Blend to a thick paste. Store in the refrigerator for 2 weeks.

Variation

For red curry paste, blend 8 sliced fresh red chillies, 15ml/1 tbsp roasted coriander seeds, 10ml/2 tsp grated fresh root ginger, 30ml/2 tbsp finely chopped lemon grass, 15ml/1 tbsp grated garlic, 3 finely chopped red shallots, the juice of 1/2 lime and 30ml/2 tbsp sunflower oil.

Energy 793kcal/3273kJ; Protein 14.7g;
Carbohydrate 27.3g, of which sugars 14.4g;
Fat 70.5g, of which saturates 8.2g; Cholesterol
0mg; Calcium 253mg; Fibre 6.1g; Sodium 45mg.

Traditional pesto

Stir this through pasta for a simple meal, or use as a base for other dishes.

INGREDIENTS

Makes approx 350ml/12fl oz/1 1/2 cups
50g/2oz fresh basil leaves
25g/1oz/1/4 cup toasted pine nuts
2 peeled garlic cloves
20ml/4fl oz/1/2 cup olive oil
25g/1oz/1/3 cup freshly grated
   Parmesan cheese
salt and ground black pepper

1 Put the basil leaves in a food processor or blender and blend to a paste with the toasted pine nuts and peeled garlic cloves. With the motor still running, drizzle in the olive oil through the feeder tube until the mixture forms a paste.

2 Spoon the pesto into a bowl and stir in the freshly grated Parmesan cheese. Season to taste with salt and ground black pepper. To store, drizzle a little oil over the top of the pesto and keep in the refrigerator for up to 1 week.

Variation

To make rocket (arugula) pesto, substitute the fresh basil leaves for 50g/2oz fresh rocket leaves and make in the same way as traditional pesto.

Energy 410kcal/1694kJ; Protein 14.9g;
Carbohydrate 2.4g, of which sugars 2.1g;
Fat 38g, of which saturates 8g; Cholesterol 25mg;
Calcium 403mg; Fibre 3g; Sodium 289mg.

Balinese spice paste

This spicy paste forms the basis of many Indonesian meat, poultry and fish dishes.

INGREDIENTS

Makes approx 250ml/8fl oz/1 cup
2 shallots, finely chopped
2 garlic cloves, finely chopped
25g/1oz fresh galangal, finely chopped
25g/1oz fresh turmeric, chopped
4 red chillies, seeded and chopped
1 lemon grass stalk, chopped
5ml/1 tsp ground coriander
2.5ml/1/2 tsp ground black pepper
30–45ml/2–3 tbsp palm oil
10ml/2 tsp shrimp paste

1 Using a mortar and pestle, grind the shallots, garlic, galangal, turmeric, chillies and lemon grass to a coarse paste. Beat in the coriander and black pepper.

2 Heat the oil in a small heavy pan, stir in the paste and fry until fragrant and beginning to colour. Stir in the shrimp paste and sugar and continue to fry for 2–3 minutes, until darker in colour. Remove from the heat and leave to cool.

3 Spoon the spice paste into a jar, cover and store in the refrigerator for up to 1 week.

Energy 158kcal/654kJ; Protein 6.6g;
Carbohydrate 8.9g, of which sugars 7.5g;
Fat 13.6g, of which saturates 1.3g; Cholesterol
25mg; Calcium 25mg; Fibre 0.8g; Sodium 355mg.

OILS IN DIPS

Oil and vinegar are the classic Mediterranean combination for dipping bread into. If you are feeling more adventurous, try mixing oil with other ingredients in one of these great recipes.

Hummus

Olive oil is an essential ingredient in this traditional Middle Eastern dip.

INGREDIENTS

Makes approx 475ml/16fl oz/2 cups
150g/5oz/³/4 cup dried chickpeas
juice of 2 lemons
2 garlic cloves, sliced
30ml/2 tbsp olive oil, plus extra for drizzling
pinch of cayenne pepper
150ml/¹/4 pint/²/3 cup tahini paste
salt and ground black pepper

1 Soak the chickpeas overnight in cold water. Drain, put in a pan and cover with fresh water. Bring to the boil and cook rapidly for 10 minutes, then simmer gently for about 1 hour, until soft. Drain.

2 Process the chickpeas in a food processor to a smooth purée. Add the lemon juice, garlic, oil, cayenne pepper and tahini and blend until creamy. Season to taste. Transfer to a serving dish and drizzle with more olive oil.

Energy 140kcal/586kJ; **Protein** 6.9g; **Carbohydrate** 11.2g, of which sugars 0.4g; **Fat** 7.8g, of which saturates 1.1g; **Cholesterol** 0mg; **Calcium** 97mg; **Fibre** 3.6g; **Sodium** 149mg.

Taramasalata

This Turkish meze favourite is often served as a dip with pitta bread.

INGREDIENTS

Makes approx 400ml/14fl oz/1²/3 cups
115g/4oz smoked mullet roe
2 garlic cloves, crushed
30ml/2 tbsp grated onion
60ml/4 tbsp olive oil
4 slices white bread, crusts removed
juice of 2 lemons
30ml/2 tbsp water
ground black pepper
warm pitta bread, to serve

1 Place the smoked fish roe, garlic, grated onion, oil, bread and lemon juice in a blender or food processor and process until smooth.

2 Add the water and process again for a few seconds. Pour into a serving bowl, cover with clear film (plastic wrap) and chill for 2 hours before sprinkling with black pepper and serving.

Energy 807kcal/3374kJ; **Protein** 36.2g; **Carbohydrate** 60.6g, of which sugars 5.4g; **Fat** 48.4g, of which saturates 7.1g; **Cholesterol** 380mg; **Calcium** 147mg; **Fibre** 3g; **Sodium** 700mg.

Tapenade

In France, tapenade is spread on bread and eaten as an hors d'oeuvre.

INGREDIENTS

Makes approx 400ml/14fl oz/1²/3 cups
225g/8oz/2 cups stoned black olives
2 large garlic cloves, peeled
15ml/1 tbsp salted capers, rinsed
6 canned or bottled anchovy fillets, drained
50g/2oz good-quality canned tuna
5ml/1 tsp chopped fresh thyme
30ml/2 tbsp chopped fresh parsley
30–60ml/2–4 tbsp olive oil
a dash of lemon juice
30ml/2 tbsp crème fraîche or fromage frais

1 Process the olives, garlic, capers, anchovies and tuna in a food processor or blender. Blend in the thyme, parsley and enough olive oil to make a paste.

2 Season to taste with pepper and a dash of lemon juice. Stir in the crème fraîche or fromage frais and transfer to a serving bowl.

Energy 157kcal/666kJ; **Protein** 6.3g; **Carbohydrate** 28.4g, of which sugars 1.8g; **Fat** 2.8g, of which saturates 0.6g; **Cholesterol** 37mg; **Calcium** 76mg; **Fibre** 1.5g; **Sodium** 523mg.

Chilli bean dip

This creamy bean dip is best served warm with triangles of toasted pitta bread.

INGREDIENTS

Serves 4

30ml/2 tbsp corn oil

2 garlic cloves, finely chopped

1 onion, finely chopped

2 green chillies, seeded and finely chopped

5–10ml/1–2 tsp hot chilli powder

400g/14oz can kidney beans

75g/3oz mature (sharp) Cheddar cheese, grated

1 red chilli, seeded and cut into strips

salt and ground black pepper

1 Heat the oil in a large frying pan and add the garlic, onion, green chillies and chilli powder. Cook for 5 minutes until the onions are softened and transparent, but not browned.

2 Drain the kidney beans, reserving the liquor. Blend all but 30ml/2 tbsp of the beans to a purée in a food processor. Add to the pan with 30ml/2 tbsp of the reserved liquor. Heat gently, mixing well.

3 Stir in the whole beans and the cheese. Cook for 3 minutes, stirring until the cheese melts. Add salt and pepper to taste. Transfer to a serving bowl. Scatter the red chilli over the top. Serve warm.

Energy 244kcal/1018kJ; **Protein** 12.7g; **Carbohydrate** 20.2g, of which sugars 4.6g; **Fat** 12.6g, of which saturates 4.8g; **Cholesterol** 18mg; **Calcium** 234mg; **Fibre** 7.1g; **Sodium** 538mg.

Chunky cherry tomato salsa

The chilli oil in this refreshing dip gives it that extra fiery edge.

INGREDIENTS

Serves 4

1 cucumber

5ml/1 tsp sea salt

500g/11/4lb cherry tomatoes, quartered

1 lemon

45ml/3 tbsp chilli oil

2.5ml/1/2 tsp dried chilli flakes

30ml/2 tbsp chopped fresh dill

1 garlic clove, finely chopped

1 Trim the ends off the cucumber and cut it into 2.5cm/1 in lengths, then cut each piece lengthways into thin slices.

2 Arrange the slices in a colander and sprinkle with sea salt. Leave for 5 minutes, then wash under cold water and dry with kitchen paper. Place in a bowl with the tomato pieces.

3 Finely grate the lemon rind and place in a small jug (pitcher) with the juice from the lemon, the chilli oil, chilli flakes, dill and garlic. Whisk with a fork.

4 Pour the chilli oil dressing over the tomato and cucumber and toss. Leave to marinate for 2 hours, then serve.

Energy 162kcal/676kJ; **Protein** 4.2g; **Carbohydrate** 16g, of which sugars 13.7g; **Fat** 9.5g, of which saturates 1.4g; **Cholesterol** 0mg; **Calcium** 83mg; **Fibre** 4.5g; **Sodium** 31mg.

Avocado and red pepper salsa

This simple salsa is a fire-and-ice mixture of hot chilli and cooling avocado.

INGREDIENTS

Serves 4

2 ripe avocados

1 red onion

1 red (bell) pepper

4 green chillies

30ml/2 tbsp chopped fresh coriander (cilantro)

20ml/2 tbsp sunflower oil

juice of 1 lemon

salt and ground black pepper

1 Halve and stone the avocados. Scoop out and finely dice the flesh. Finely chop the red onion.

2 Slice the top off the pepper and pull out the central core. Shake out any remaining seeds. Cut the pepper into thin strips and then into fine dice.

3 Halve the chillies, remove their seeds and finely chop the flesh. Mix the chillies, coriander, oil, lemon and salt and pepper to taste.

4 Place the avocado, red onion and pepper in a bowl. Pour in the chilli and coriander dressing and toss the mixture well. Serve immediately.

Energy 216kcal/890kJ; **Protein** 2.4g; **Carbohydrate** 5.8g, of which sugars 4.2g; **Fat** 20.3g, of which saturates 3.8g; **Cholesterol** 0mg; **Calcium** 41mg; **Fibre** 4.1g; **Sodium** 11mg.

OILS IN SOUPS

Whether as a base for rich vegetable soups or as a finishing touch to add flavour, oils are an essential ingredient in these delicious, warming recipes.

White radish and beef soup

The smoky flavours of beef are perfectly complemented by the tanginess of Chinese white radish in this mild and refreshing soup with a slightly sweet edge.

INGREDIENTS

Serves 4

200g/7oz Chinese white radish, peeled

50g/2oz beef, chopped into bitesize cubes

15ml/1 tbsp sesame oil

¹/₂ leek, sliced

15ml/1 tbsp soy sauce

salt and ground black pepper

1 Slice the white radish and cut the pieces into 2cm/³/₄in squares.

2 Heat the sesame oil in a large pan and stir-fry the beef until golden brown. Add the white radish and briefly stir-fry.

3 Add 750ml/1¹/₄ pints/3 cups water. Boil, then simmer, covered, for 7 minutes. Add the leek, soy sauce and seasoning. Simmer for 2 minutes. Serve.

Energy 60kcal/247kJ; **Protein** 3.7g; **Carbohydrate** 2g, of which sugars 1.8g; **Fat** 4.1, of which saturates 1g; **Cholesterol** 7mg; **Calcium** 17mg; **Fibre** 1g; **Sodium** 281mg.

Tomato, ciabatta and basil oil soup

Basil oil captures the delicate flavour of this classic Italian herb and makes a simple tomato soup something special.

INGREDIENTS

Serves 4

45ml/3 tbsp olive oil

1 red onion, chopped

6 garlic cloves, chopped

300ml/¹/₂ pint/1¹/₄ cups white wine

150ml/¹/₄ pint/²/₃ cup water

12 plum tomatoes, quartered

2 x 400g/14oz cans plum tomatoes

2.5ml/¹/₂ tsp sugar

¹/₂ ciabatta loaf

salt and ground black pepper

basil leaves, to garnish

120ml/4fl oz/¹/₂ cup basil oil

1 Heat the oil in a large pan and cook the onion and garlic for 4–5 minutes until softened.

2 Add the wine, water, fresh and canned tomatoes. Bring to the boil, reduce the heat and cover the pan, then simmer for 3–4 minutes. Add the sugar and season well with salt and black pepper.

3 Break the bread into bitesize pieces and stir into the soup.

4 Ladle the soup into bowls. Garnish with basil and drizzle the basil oil over each portion.

Energy 332kcal/1396kJ; **Protein** 7.8g; **Carbohydrate** 35.4g, of which sugars 16.3g; **Fat** 13.4g, of which saturates 2g; **Cholesterol** 0mg; **Calcium** 98mg; **Fibre** 5g; **Sodium** 306mg.

Peanut and potato soup

This soup is wonderfully warming.
Serve with peanuts for added crunch.

INGREDIENTS

Serves 6

1 onion, finely chopped

60ml/4 tbsp groundnut (peanut) oil

2 garlic cloves, crushed

1 red (bell) pepper, seeded and chopped

250g/9oz potatoes, peeled and diced

2 fresh red chillies, seeded and chopped

200g/7oz canned chopped tomatoes

150g/5oz/1¼ cups unsalted peanuts

1.5 litres/2½ pints/6¼ cups beef stock

salt and ground black pepper

1 Cook the onion in the oil for 5 minutes,
until beginning to soften. Add the garlic,
pepper, potatoes, chillies and tomatoes.
Stir well to coat the vegetables evenly in
the oil, cover and cook for 5 minutes.

2 Toast the peanuts in a dry frying pan.
Set 30ml/2 tbsp of the peanuts aside.
Transfer the remaining peanuts to a food
processor and process until finely
ground. Add the vegetables and process
again until smooth.

3 Return to the pan and stir in the beef
stock. Bring to the boil, lower the heat
and simmer for 10 minutes. Serve
garnished with the remaining peanuts.

Energy 260kcal/1079kJ; **Protein** 8g;
Carbohydrate 14.7g, of which sugars 6.2g;
Fat 19.2g, of which saturates 3.6g; **Cholesterol**
0mg; **Calcium** 30mg; **Fibre** 3g; **Sodium** 20mg.

Crab, coconut and coriander soup

This South American soup combines the
distinctive flavours of creamy coconut,
palm oil, fragrant coriander and chilli.

INGREDIENTS

Serves 4

30ml/2 tbsp olive oil

1 onion, finely chopped

1 celery stick, finely chopped

2 garlic cloves, crushed

1 fresh chilli, seeded and chopped

1 large tomato, peeled and chopped

45ml/3 tbsp chopped fresh coriander (cilantro)

1 litre/1¾ pints/4 cups fresh fish stock

500g/1¼lb crab meat

250ml/8fl oz/1 cup coconut milk

30ml/2 tbsp palm oil

juice of 1 lime

salt

hot chilli oil and lime wedges to serve

1 Heat the olive oil in a pan over a low
heat. Stir in the onion and celery and
sauté gently for 5 minutes until
softened and translucent. Stir in the
garlic and chilli and cook for 2 minutes.

2 Add the tomato and half the coriander
and increase the heat. Cook, stirring, for
3 minutes, then add the stock. Bring to
the boil, then simmer for 5 minutes.

3 Stir the crab, coconut milk and
palm oil into the pan and simmer
over a very low heat for a further
5 minutes. The consistency should be
thick, but not stew-like, so add some
water if needed.

4 Stir in the lime juice and remaining
coriander, then season with salt to taste.
Serve in heated bowls with the chilli oil
and lime wedges to serve.

Energy 228kcal/951kJ; **Protein** 23.6g;
Carbohydrate 5.4g, of which sugars 5g; **Fat** 12.6g,
of which saturates 3.7g; **Cholesterol** 90mg;
Calcium 199mg; **Fibre** 1.1g; **Sodium** 767mg.

OILS IN SALADS

Oil is the classic dressing ingredient for salads. These recipes often use olive oil, but you could also try a home-flavoured herb oil or a more distinctive nut oil.

Tomato salad with marinated peppers and oregano

The simple combination of olive oil and white wine vinegar is used to dress this classic summer salad.

INGREDIENTS

Serves 2–4

2 marinated (bell) peppers, drained

6 ripe tomatoes, sliced

15ml/1 tbsp chopped fresh oregano

75ml/5 tbsp olive oil

30ml/2 tbsp white wine vinegar

sea salt

Roasted red peppers with feta, capers and preserved lemons

The Mediterranean flavours of this dish cry out for the distinctive taste of argan oil, but you can use olive oil too.

INGREDIENTS

Serves 4

4 red (bell) peppers

200g /7oz feta cheese, crumbled

30–45ml/2–3 tbsp argan oil or olive oil

30ml/2tbsp capers

peel of 1 preserved lemon, cut into
  small pieces

salt (optional)

1 Preheat the grill (broiler) on the hottest setting. Roast the red peppers under the grill, turning frequently, until they soften and their skins begin to blacken.

2 Place the peppers in a plastic bag, seal and leave them to stand for 15 minutes.

3 Peel the peppers, remove the stalks and seeds, then slice the flesh and arrange on a plate.

4 Add the crumbled feta and pour over the argan oil or olive oil.

5 Scatter the capers and preserved lemon over the top and sprinkle with a little salt, if required (this depends on whether the feta is salty or not). Serve with chunks of fresh bread to mop up the delicious, oil-rich juices.

Energy 233kcal/967kJ; **Protein** 9.8g;
Carbohydrate 12.2g, of which sugars 11.6g; **Fat** 16.4g, of which saturates 7.8g; **Cholesterol** 35mg; **Calcium** 209mg; **Fibre** 3.2g; **Sodium** 730mg.

1 Cut the marinated peppers into strips. Arrange the tomato slices and pepper strips on a serving dish, sprinkle with the oregano and season to taste with sea salt.

2 Whisk together the olive oil and vinegar in a jug (pitcher) and pour over the salad. Serve immediately or cover and chill in the refrigerator until required.

Energy 119kcal/494kJ; **Protein** 1.4g;
Carbohydrate 6.9g, of which sugars 6.7g;
Fat 9.7g, of which saturates 1.5g; **Cholesterol** 0mg; **Calcium** 17mg; **Fibre** 2.1g; **Sodium** 12mg.

Stilton and walnut salad

The addition of walnut oil in the dressing gives this simple salad a really rich, nutty flavour.

INGREDIENTS

Serves 4

mixed salad leaves

4 fresh figs

115g/4 oz stilton, cut into small chunks

75g/3oz/³⁄₄ cup walnut halves

For the dressing

45ml/3 tbsp walnut oil

juice of 1 lemon

salt and ground black pepper

1 Mix all the dressing ingredients together in a bowl. Whisk briskly until thick and emulsified.

2 Wash and dry the salad leaves, then tear them gently into bitesize pieces. Place in a mixing bowl and toss with the dressing. Transfer to a large serving dish.

3 Cut the figs into quarters and add to the salad leaves. Sprinkle the cheese over, crumbling it slightly. Then sprinkle over the walnuts, breaking them up roughly with your fingers as you go.

Energy 415kcal/1726kJ; **Protein** 10.6g; **Carbohydrate** 26.6g, of which sugars 26.4g; **Fat** 30.3g, of which saturates 7.3g; **Cholesterol** 22mg; **Fibre** 4.5g; **Sodium** 383mg.

Bulgur wheat salad

This traditional meze dish of bulgur and tomato is easy to make and delicious. Olive oil adds to the mix of flavours and stops the dish being too dry.

INGREDIENTS

Serves 4–6

175g/6oz/1 cup bulgur wheat, rinsed
  and drained

45–60ml/3–4 tbsp olive oil

juice of 1–2 lemons

30ml/2 tbsp tomato purée (paste)

10ml/2 tsp sugar

1 large or 2 small red onions, cut in half
  lengthways, in half again crossways, and
  sliced along the grain

1–2 fresh red chillies, seeded and
  finely chopped

1 bunch each of fresh mint and flat leaf
  parsley, finely chopped

salt and ground black pepper

a few fresh mint and parsley leaves,
  to garnish

1 Put the bulgur into a wide bowl, pour over enough boiling water to cover it by about 2.5cm/1in, and give it a quick stir.

2 Cover the bowl with a plate or pan lid and leave the bulgur to steam for about 25 minutes, until it has soaked up the water and doubled in quantity.

3 Pour the oil and lemon juice over the bulgur and toss to mix, then add the tomato purée and toss the mixture again until the bulgur is well coated.

4 Add the sugar, onion, red chillies and the herbs. Season with salt and pepper.

5 Serve at room temperature, garnished with a little mint and parsley.

Energy 149kcal/620kJ; **Protein** 3g; **Carbohydrate** 21.6g, of which sugars 5.4g; **Fat** 6.1g, of which saturates 0.8g; **Cholesterol** 0mg; **Calcium** 54mg; **Fibre** 1.7g; **Sodium** 19mg.

OILS IN DEEP-FRIED SAVOURY DISHES

Use an oil that can withstand high temperatures for deep-frying, such as sunflower or groundnut (peanut) oil. If food is fried in oil that is not hot enough, it will become soggy.

Japanese tempura

In this classic dish from Japan, ingredients such as prawns and vegetables are coated in a light batter and deep-fried very briefly in sunflower or groundnut oil.

INGREDIENTS

Serves 4

50g/2oz/$\frac{1}{2}$ cup rice flour

100g/3$\frac{3}{4}$oz/scant 1 cup plain
   (all-purpose) flour

2.5ml/$\frac{1}{2}$ tsp baking powder

2 large (US extra large) egg whites, beaten

350–400ml/12–14fl oz/1$\frac{1}{2}$–1$\frac{2}{3}$ cup
   ice-cold soda water (club soda)

sunflower oil, or groundnut (peanut) oil
   for deep-frying

8 raw tiger prawns (jumbo shrimp),
   peeled, with tails intact

300g/11oz assorted vegetables, such as
   sliced sweet potato, broccoli florets, baby
   spinach leaves, courgette (zucchini) slices,
   sliced red and yellow (bell) pepper

1 Preheat the oven to low. Mix the flours, baking powder, beaten egg whites and soda water and stir until just combined. (Do not overmix or the batter will become heavy. It should be lumpy.)

2 Pour the oil into a wok to a depth of 7.5cm/3in and heat to 180°C/350°F. Working in batches, dip the prawns and vegetables in the batter, shaking off the excess batter, and deep-fry for 3 minutes, or until golden.

3 Drain the tempura on a wire rack lined with kitchen paper, then transfer to another wire rack (with no paper) and place in the oven to keep warm. Cook the remaining tempura and serve immediately with dipping sauce.

Energy 669kcal/2,775kJ; **Protein** 48.7g; **Carbohydrate** 5g, of which sugars 3.8g; **Fat** 45.9g, of which saturates 11.1g; **Cholesterol** 250mg; **Calcium** 37mg; **Fibre** 0.9g; **Sodium** 196mg.

Prawn and sesame toasts

These little toasts are quickly fried in oil.

INGREDIENTS

Serves 4

225g/8oz peeled raw prawns (shrimp)

15ml/1 tbsp sherry

15ml/1 tbsp soy sauce

30ml/2 tbsp cornflour (cornstarch)

2 egg whites

4 slices white bread, cut into quarters

115g/4oz/$\frac{1}{2}$ cup sesame seeds

groundnut (peanut) oil, or sunflower oil
   for deep-frying

1 Process the prawns, sherry, soy sauce and cornflour in a food processor. Whisk the egg whites until stiff. Fold them into the prawn and cornflour mixture.

2 Put the sesame seeds on to a plate. Spread the prawn paste over one side of each bread triangle, then press into the sesame seeds. Heat the oil in a wok to 190°C/375°F. Add the toasts, prawn side down, and deep-fry for 2 minutes, then turn and fry on the other side until golden. Drain on kitchen paper and serve.

Energy 433kcal/1,806kJ; **Protein** 19.1g; **Carbohydrate** 27.7g, of which sugars 1.2g; **Fat** 27.6g, of which saturates 3.6g; **Cholesterol** 110mg; **Calcium** 271mg; **Fibre** 2.7g; **Sodium** 559mg.

Chips (French fries)

These chips are fried twice in oil – once to cook them and then a second time to brown them and give them a crispy coating.

INGREDIENTS

Serves 4

groundnut (peanut) or sunflower oil, for frying

675g/1¹/₂lb potatoes

salt

1 Heat the oil to 150°C/300°F. Peel the potatoes and cut them into chips (fries) about 1cm/¹/₂in thick. Rinse and dry.

2 Lower a batch of chips into the hot oil and cook for about 5 minutes or until tender but not browned.

3 Lift out the chips with a slotted spoon, place on kitchen paper and leave to cool.

4 Just before serving, increase the temperature of the oil to 190°C/375°F. Add the par-cooked chips, in batches.

5 Cook until crisp, then lift out and drain on kitchen paper.

6 Sprinkle with salt and serve at once.

Energy 403kcal/1689kJ; **Protein** 5.4g; **Carbohydrate** 51.5g, of which sugars 2.9g; **Fat** 14.5g, of which saturates 6.1g; **Cholesterol** 0mg; **Calcium** 19mg; **Fibre** 3.7g; **Sodium** 59mg.

Deep-fried wontons

When frying the wontons, make sure your oil is not too hot – they will scorch.

INGREDIENTS

Serves 4

300g/11oz/1¹/₂ cups minced (ground) pork

15ml/1 tbsp light soy sauce

15ml/1 tbsp sesame oil

2.5ml/¹/₂ tsp ground black pepper

15ml/1 tbsp cornflour (cornstarch)

16 wonton wrappers

groundnut (peanut) oil or sunflower oil, for deep-frying

chilli dipping sauce, to serve

1 Put the minced pork in a bowl. Add the light soy sauce, sesame oil, ground black pepper and cornflour. Mix well.

2 Place about 5ml/1 tsp of the mixture in the centre of a wonton wrapper, bring the corners together so that they meet at the top, and pinch the neck to seal. Fill the remaining wontons in the same way.

3 Heat the groundnut or sunflower oil in a wok or deep-fryer. Carefully add the filled wontons, about four or five at a time, and deep-fry until golden brown.

4 Carefully lift out the cooked wontons with a slotted spoon, drain on kitchen paper and keep hot while frying successive batches. Serve the wontons hot with chilli dipping sauce.

Energy 326kcal/1357kJ; **Protein** 16.3g; **Carbohydrate** 18.3g, of which sugars 0.6g; **Fat** 21.3g, of which saturates 4.4g; **Cholesterol** 50mg; **Calcium** 33mg; **Fibre** 0.6g; **Sodium** 319mg.

OILS IN DEEP-FRIED SWEET DISHES

Deep-frying food gives it a crispy finish while allowing the centre of the food to stay soft – which makes it an ideal cooking technique for these sweet dishes.

Cinnamon and apple fritters

Served piping hot with a dollop of crème fraîche, these slices of crisp apple in a fluffy, cinnamon-scented batter will fill the house with a mouth-watering aroma. Preserve the flavour and lightness of the batter by deep-frying the fritters in very hot vegetable oil.

INGREDIENTS

Serves 4–6

3–4 tart eating apples such as Granny Smith

50ml/2fl oz/$^{1}/_{4}$ cup Marsala

3 eggs, beaten

125g/4$^{1}/_{4}$oz/generous 1 cup plain (all-purpose) flour

30g/1$^{1}/_{4}$oz/generous 2 tbsp golden caster (superfine) sugar

5ml/1 tsp ground cinnamon

2.5ml/$^{1}/_{2}$ tsp salt

vegetable oil, for deep-frying

berries, to decorate

caster (superfine) sugar, for dusting

crème fraîche, to serve

1 Peel, core and slice the apple into 1cm/$^{1}/_{2}$in rings. Place the apple slices in a large, shallow bowl and pour over the Marsala, turning to coat them evenly. Cover and set aside to macerate for about 1 hour.

2 Beat together the eggs, flour, sugar, cinnamon and salt in a large bowl until thick and smooth. Drain the apples and set aside, reserving the Marsala. Add enough of the Marsala to the batter to make a coating consistency. Beat until smooth and free of lumps.

3 Add the apples to the batter and stir gently to coat evenly. Heat the oil in a deep-fat fryer or a large, heavy pan to 180°C/350°F.

4 Working in batches, lower the apple rings into the oil and deep-fry for 3–4 minutes until golden. Remove with a slotted spoon and drain on a wire rack placed over crumpled kitchen paper. Divide the fritters among warmed serving plates and decorate with berries. Dust with caster sugar and serve immediately with crème fraîche.

Energy 286kcal/1195kJ; **Protein** 5.4g; **Carbohydrate** 29.9g, of which sugars 14g; **Fat** 16g, of which saturates 2.2g; **Cholesterol** 95mg; **Calcium** 50mg; **Fibre** 2g; **Sodium** 38mg.

American-style sugared donuts

These irresistible, all-time favourite treats are cooked without yeast for a shorter preparation time and almost instant results.

INGREDIENTS

Serves 4

60g/2¹/₄oz/generous 4 tbsp unsalted butter

60g/2¹/₄oz/generous ¹/₄ cup caster (superfine) sugar

1 large (US extra large) egg, beaten

90ml/6 tbsp buttermilk

225g/8oz/2 cups plain (all-purpose) flour

5ml/1 tsp baking powder

2.5ml/¹/₂ tsp bicarbonate of soda (baking soda)

pinch of salt

finely grated rind of 1 orange

5ml/1 tsp ground cinnamon

pinch of grated nutmeg

vegetable oil, for deep-frying

icing (confectioners') sugar, for dusting

1 Place the butter, sugar, beaten egg and buttermilk in a large bowl.

2 Sift over the flour, baking powder, bicarbonate of soda and salt.

3 Add the orange rind, cinnamon and nutmeg and mix using a wooden spoon until well-mixed and smooth.

4 Turn the mixture out on to a lightly floured work surface. With floured hands, knead the dough for about 5 minutes until it becomes really smooth and slightly soft and elastic but not sticky.

5 Roll out the dough on a lightly floured surface to 1.5cm/²/₃in thick and stamp out rounds using a 5cm/2in cutter. Press a hole through each one with the handle of a wooden spoon to make a ring shape.

6 Pour the oil into a deep fat fryer, wok or a large, heavy pan and heat to 180°C/350°F.

7 Fry the donuts, in batches, for about 5 minutes, or until browned and cooked through. Lift out with a skimmer and drain on a wire rack lined with kitchen paper. Leave to cool slightly, then dust with sifted icing sugar and serve warm.

Energy 192kcal/801kJ; **Protein** 2.5g; **Carbohydrate** 22.6g, of which sugars 8.3g; **Fat** 10.8g, of which saturates 1.4g; **Cholesterol** 16mg; **Calcium** 37mg; **Fibre** 0.6g; **Sodium** 11mg.

Deep-fried cherries

Crispy on the outside, soft in the middle, these cherries make an unusual dessert.

INGREDIENTS

Serves 4–6

450g/1lb ripe red cherries, on their stalks

120g/4¹/₄oz/generous 1 cup plain (all-purpose) flour

60g/2¹/₄oz/generous ¹/₄ cup golden caster (superfine) sugar

75ml/5 tbsp full-fat (whole) milk

75ml/5 tbsp dry white wine

3 eggs, beaten

vegetable oil, for deep-frying

icing (confectioners') sugar and ground cinnamon, for dusting

1 Wash and dry the cherries. Tie the stalks together into clusters of 4–5 cherries. Place the flour, golden caster sugar, milk, white wine and eggs in a bowl and mix to make a smooth batter. Pour the vegetable oil into a deep-fat fryer or pan and heat to 190°C/375°F.

2 Working in batches, half-dip each cherry cluster into the batter and then carefully drop the cluster into the hot oil. Fry for 3–4 minutes until golden. Remove the cherries with a slotted spoon and drain on a wire rack placed over kitchen paper.

3 Dust the cherries with icing sugar and cinnamon and serve with ice cream.

Energy 201kcal/840kJ; **Protein** 3.7g; **Carbohydrate** 25.7g, of which sugars 7.3g; **Fat** 10g, of which saturates 1.3g; **Cholesterol** 26mg; **Calcium** 46mg; **Fibre** 1.3g; **Sodium** 11mg.

OILS IN STIR-FRIED DISHES

Oriental cuisine is so healthy because it involves frying ingredients in small amounts of hot oil to preserve the nutrients and keep the final dish light and crisp.

Duck and sesame stir-fry

This stir-fry is cooked using a mixture of half-and-half sesame and vegetable oil.

INGREDIENTS

Serves 4

15ml/1 tbsp sesame oil

15ml/1 tbsp vegetable oil

4 garlic cloves, finely sliced

250g/9oz duck meat, cut into bitesize pieces

2.5ml/1/2 tsp dried chilli flakes

15ml/1 tbsp Thai fish sauce (nam pla)

15ml/1 tbsp light soy sauce

120ml/4fl oz/1/2 cup water

1 head broccoli, cut into small florets

coriander (cilantro) and 15ml/1 tbsp toasted
  sesame seeds, to garnish

1 Heat the oils in a wok and gently stir-fry the garlic until it is golden brown. Add the duck and stir-fry for a further 2 minutes, until it begins to brown.

2 Stir in the chilli flakes, fish sauce, soy sauce and water. Add the broccoli and continue to stir-fry for 2 minutes, until the duck is cooked through. Serve garnished with coriander and sesame seeds.

Energy 192kcal/798kJ; **Protein** 18.7g;
Carbohydrate 2.7g, of which sugars 2.3g; **Fat**
12.9g, of which saturates 2.1g; **Cholesterol** 69mg;
Calcium 104mg; **Fibre** 3.6g; **Sodium** 436mg.

Celebration noodles

Stir-fry the ingredients in this noodle dish in palm or coconut oil for an authentic Filipino taste.

INGREDIENTS

Serves 4

30ml/2 tbsp palm or coconut oil

1 large onion, finely chopped

2–3 garlic cloves, finely chopped

250g/9oz pork loin, cut into thin strips

250g/9oz fresh shelled shrimps

2 carrots, cut into matchsticks

1/2 small green cabbage, finely shredded

250ml/8fl oz/ 1 cup pork or chicken stock

50ml/2fl oz/1/4 cup soy sauce

15ml/1 tbsp palm sugar (jaggery)

450g/1lb fresh egg noodles

2 hard-boiled eggs, finely chopped

1 lime, quartered

1 Heat 15ml/1 tbsp oil in a wok, stir in the onion and garlic and fry until fragrant and beginning to colour.

2 Toss in the pork and shrimp and stir-fry for 2 minutes, then transfer the mixture on to a plate.

3 Return the wok to the heat, add the remaining oil, then stir in the carrots and cabbage and stir-fry for 2–3 minutes. Transfer the vegetables on to the plate with the pork and shrimp.

4 Pour the stock, soy sauce and sugar into the wok and stir until the sugar has dissolved. Add the noodles and cook for about 3 minutes, until tender but still firm to the bite. Toss in the pork, shrimp, cabbage and carrots, mixing thoroughly.

5 Transfer the noodles on to a serving dish and scatter the chopped eggs over the top. Serve immediately with the lime wedges.

Energy 728kcal/3069kJ; **Protein** 43.6g;
Carbohydrate 98g, of which sugars 16.9g; **Fat**
20.8g, of which saturates 5g; **Cholesterol** 290mg;
Calcium 159mg; **Fibre** 6.3g; **Sodium** 1303mg.

Thai fried rice

This dish uses two different flavoured oils. The ingredients are first stir-fried in groundnut oil, while a small amount of hot and spicy chilli oil is added as a last minute condiment.

INGREDIENTS

Serves 4

475ml/16fl oz/2 cups water

50g/2oz/¹/₂ cup coconut milk powder

350g/12oz/1³/₄ cups Thai jasmine
  rice, rinsed

30ml/2 tbsp groundnut (peanut) oil

2 garlic cloves, chopped

1 small onion, finely chopped

2.5cm/1in piece fresh root ginger, peeled
  and grated

225g/8oz skinned chicken breast fillets, cut
  into 1cm/¹/₂in pieces

1 red (bell) pepper, seeded and sliced

115g/4oz/1 cup drained canned whole
  kernel corn

5ml/1 tsp chilli oil

5ml/1 tsp hot curry powder

2 eggs, beaten

salt

spring onion (scallion) shreds, to garnish

1 Pour the water into a pan and whisk in the coconut milk powder. Add the rice and bring to the boil. Reduce the heat, cover and cook for 12 minutes, or until the rice is tender and the liquid has been absorbed. Spread the rice on a baking sheet and leave until cold.

2 Heat the groundnut oil in a wok, add the garlic, onion and ginger and stir-fry over a medium heat for 2 minutes.

3 Push the onion mixture to the sides of the wok, add the chicken to the centre and stir-fry for 2 minutes. Add the rice and toss well. Stir-fry over a high heat for about 3 minutes more, until the chicken is cooked through.

4 Stir in the sliced red pepper, corn, chilli oil and curry powder, with salt to taste. Toss over the heat for 1 minute. Stir in the beaten eggs and cook for 1 minute more. Garnish with the spring onion shreds and serve.

Energy 669kcal/2,775kJ; **Protein** 48.7g; **Carbohydrate** 5g, of which sugars 3.8g; **Fat** 45.9g, of which saturates 11.1g; **Cholesterol** 250mg; **Calcium** 37mg; **Fibre** 0.9g; **Sodium** 196mg.

Stir-fried pork with dried shrimp

Classic Chinese ingredients are stir-fried in vegetable oil.

INGREDIENTS

Serves 4

250g/9oz pork fillet (tenderloin), sliced

30ml/2 tbsp vegetable oil

2 garlic cloves, finely chopped

45ml/3 tbsp dried shrimp

10ml/2 tsp dried shrimp paste

30ml/2 tbsp soy sauce

juice of 1 lime

15ml/1 tbsp light muscovado (brown) sugar

1 small fresh red or green chilli, seeded and
  finely chopped

4 pak choi (bok choy), shredded

1 Place the pork in the freezer for 30 minutes, until firm. Cut it into thin slices.

2 Heat the oil in a wok or frying pan and cook the garlic until golden brown. Add the pork and stir-fry for about 4 minutes, until just cooked through.

3 Add the dried shrimp, then stir in the shrimp paste, with the soy sauce, lime juice and sugar.

4 Add the chilli and pak choi and toss over the heat until the vegetables are just wilted. Transfer to individual bowls and serve immediately.

Energy 200kcal/833kJ; **Protein** 23.1g; **Carbohydrate** 6.3g, of which sugars 6.2g; **Fat** 9.2g, of which saturates 1.7g; **Cholesterol** 96mg; **Calcium** 334mg; **Fibre** 2.4g; **Sodium** 1,223mg.

OILS IN SHALLOW-FRIED DISHES

Cooking quickly, slowly or sautéing, shallow-frying is a very versatile kitchen technique which is used in many favourite dishes from all around the world.

Asian-style crab cakes

Shallow-frying these crab cakes gives them a lovely crispy finish.

INGREDIENTS

Makes 16

450g/1lb/2²/₃ cups fresh crab meat

15ml/1 tbsp grated fresh root ginger

15–30ml/1–2 tbsp plain (all-purpose) flour

60ml/4 tbsp groundnut (peanut) or
    sunflower oil

salt and ground black pepper

1 Put the crab meat in a bowl with the ginger, salt and ground black pepper and flour. Stir well until mixed. Using floured hands, divide into 16 equal-sized pieces and shape roughly into patties.

2 Heat the oil in a frying pan and add the patties, four at a time. Cook for 3 minutes on each side, until golden. Remove with a metal spatula and leave to drain on kitchen paper for a few minutes.

3 Keep warm while you cook the remaining patties in the same way. Serve.

Energy 67kcal/280kJ; **Protein** 5.7g; **Carbohydrate** 1.5g, of which sugars 0g; **Fat** 4.3g, of which saturates 0.5g; **Cholesterol** 20mg; **Calcium** 3mg; **Fibre** 0.1g; **Sodium** 119mg.

Meatballs in rich tomato sauce

This dish is an Italian favourite. Simmering the meatballs in a rich, oil-based sauce keeps them mouth-wateringly tender.

INGREDIENTS

Serves 4

500g/1¼lb minced (ground) beef or lamb

1 onion, grated

1 egg, lightly beaten

50g/2oz/generous ¹/₃ cup short
    grain rice

45ml/3 tbsp chopped flat leaf parsley

finely grated rind of ¹/₂ orange, plus extra
    to garnish (optional)

salt and ground black pepper

For the sauce

60ml/4 tbsp extra virgin olive oil

1 onion, thinly sliced

3–4 fresh sage leaves, finely sliced

400g/14oz can tomatoes

300ml/¹/₂ pint/1¹/₄ cups beef stock

1 Put the meat in a bowl and add the onion, egg, rice and parsley. Add the grated orange rind with the salt and pepper. Mix all the ingredients well, then shape the mixture into round balls.

2 Make the sauce. Heat the oil in a wide pan that will take the meatballs in one layer. Sauté the onion slices until they are golden. Add the sage, then the tomatoes, breaking them up with a wooden spoon.

3 Simmer for a few minutes, then add the stock and bring to the boil. Lower the meatballs into the sauce. Do not stir but rotate the pan to coat evenly. Season, cover the pan and simmer for 30 minutes until the sauce has thickened. Scatter over a little orange rind to garnish, if you like.

Energy 475kcal/1972kJ; **Protein** 28.5g; **Carbohydrate** 15.8g, of which sugars 5.1g; **Fat** 33.2g, of which saturates 10.7g; **Cholesterol** 123mg; **Calcium** 58mg; **Fibre** 2g; **Sodium** 131mg.

Flash-fried squid

Squid is first marinaded then fried
very quickly in olive oil.

INGREDIENTS

Serves 6–8

500g/1¼lb very small squid, cleaned

90ml/6 tbsp olive oil, plus extra

1 red chilli, seeded and finely chopped

10ml/2 tsp Spanish smoked paprika (pimentón)

30ml/2 tbsp plain (all-purpose) flour

2 garlic cloves, finely chopped

15ml/1 tbsp sherry vinegar

5ml/1 tsp grated lemon rind

30–45ml/2–3 tbsp finely chopped fresh parsley

1 Cut the squid body sacs into rings and
the tentacles into bitesize pieces. Place in
a bowl and add 30ml/2 tbsp of the oil,
half the chilli and the paprika. Season,
cover and marinate for 2 hours.

2 Toss the squid in the flour and divide
it into 2 batches. Heat the remaining
oil in a wok. Add the first batch
of squid and fry for 2 minutes, until
the squid becomes opaque and the
tentacles have curled. Sprinkle in half
the garlic. Stir, then turn out on to a plate.

3 Repeat with the second batch.
Sprinkle over the sherry vinegar, lemon
rind, remaining chilli and parsley. Serve.

Energy 139kcal/580kJ; **Protein** 10.1g;
Carbohydrate 3.8g, of which sugars 0.1g; **Fat** 9.4g,
of which saturates 1.4g; **Cholesterol** 141mg;
Calcium 21mg; **Fibre** 0.3g; **Sodium** 70mg.

Griddled beef with sesame

In this Korean dish, thin strips of sirloin
are marinated in sesame oil and soy
sauce, then cooked in a griddle pan.

INGREDIENTS

Serves 4

800g/1¾lb sirloin steak

For the marinade

4 spring onions (scallions)

½ onion

1 Asian pear

60ml/4 tbsp dark soy sauce

60ml/4 tbsp sugar

30ml/2 tbsp sesame oil

10ml/2 tsp ground black pepper

5ml/1 tsp sesame seeds

2 garlic cloves, crushed

15ml/1 tbsp lemonade

1 Finely slice the steak, and tenderize
by bashing with a meat mallet. Cut
into bitesize strips.

2 Shred one of the spring onions and
set aside for a garnish. Finely slice
the remaining spring onions, the onion
and pear.

3 Combine all the marinade ingredients
in a large bowl to form a paste, adding
a little water if necessary.

4 Mix the beef in with the marinade,
making sure that it is well coated. Leave
in the refrigerator for at least 30
minutes or up to 2 hours (if left longer
the meat will become too salty).

5 Heat a griddle pan gently. Add the
meat and cook over a medium heat.
Once the meat is cooked through,
transfer it to a large serving dish, garnish
with the spring onion and serve.

Energy 330kcal/1382kJ; **Protein** 47.3g;
Carbohydrate 8.2g, of which sugars 8.1g; **Fat** 12.1g,
of which saturates 4.5g; **Cholesterol** 102mg;
Calcium 22mg; **Fibre** 0.2g; **Sodium** 141mg.

OILS IN GRILLED DISHES

Use oil for marinading meat or fish before cooking, or brush with oil before grilling to stop food drying out. Basting with oil during cooking will keep meat tender.

Monkfish kebabs

In this recipe, monkfish is marinated in a mixture of olive oil and lemon juice.

INGREDIENTS

Serves 4

900g/2lb fresh monkfish tail, skinned

3 (bell) peppers, red, green and yellow

juice of 1 lemon

60ml/4 tbsp olive oil

salt and ground black pepper

1 Trim the skinned monkfish and cut it into bitesize cubes. Cut each pepper into quarters, and then seed and halve each quarter. Combine the lemon juice and oil in a bowl and add seasoning.

2 Marinate the fish and pepper in the mixture for 20 minutes. Soak four wooden skewers in cold water for 30 minutes to prevent them burning during cooking.

3 Preheat a very hot grill (broiler). Thread pieces of fish and pepper alternately. Cook for 10 minutes, turning and basting frequently. Serve in pitta bread, with a squeeze of fresh lemon juice.

Energy 377kcal/1,586kJ; **Protein** 37.4g; **Carbohydrate** 24.1g, of which sugars 23.1g; **Fat** 15.3g, of which saturates 2.4g; **Cholesterol** 32mg; **Calcium** 54mg; **Fibre** 2.8g; **Sodium** 382mg.

Grilled hake with lemon and chilli

The oil in this dish infuses the fish with the flavours of chilli and lemon rind.

INGREDIENTS

Serves 4

4 hake fillets, each 150g/5oz

30ml/2 tbsp olive oil

finely grated rind and juice
  of 1 unwaxed lemon

15ml/1 tbsp crushed chilli flakes

salt and ground black pepper

1 Preheat the grill (broiler) to high. Brush the hake fillets all over with the olive oil and place them skin side up on a baking sheet.

2 Grill (broil) the fish for 4–5 minutes, until the skin is crispy, then carefully turn them over using a metal spatula.

3 Sprinkle the fillets with the lemon rind and chilli flakes and season with salt and ground black pepper.

4 Grill the fillets for a further 2–3 minutes, or until the hake is cooked through. (Test using the point of a sharp knife; the flesh should flake.) Squeeze over the lemon juice just before serving.

Energy 206kcal/862kJ; **Protein** 27g; **Carbohydrate** 0g, of which sugars 0g; **Fat** 11g, of which saturates 2g; **Cholesterol** 35mg; **Calcium** 26mg; **Fibre** 0g; **Sodium** 300mg.

Fragrant grilled chicken

The sesame oil marinade adds flavour to this delicately-spiced chicken. Basting the chicken with the marinade mixture halfway through cooking will ensure that the chicken remains tender and full of flavour.

INGREDIENTS

Serves 4

450g/1lb boneless chicken breast portions, with the skin on

30ml/2 tbsp sesame oil

2 garlic cloves, crushed

2 coriander (cilantro) roots, finely chopped

2 small fresh red chillies, seeded and finely chopped

30ml/2 tbsp Thai fish sauce (nam pla)

5ml/1 tsp sugar

cooked rice, to serve

lime wedges, to garnish

For the sauce

90ml/6 tbsp rice vinegar

60ml/4 tbsp sugar

2.5ml/1/2 tsp salt

2 garlic cloves, crushed

1 small fresh red chilli, seeded and finely chopped

115g/4oz/4 cups fresh coriander (cilantro), finely chopped

1 Lay the chicken between two sheets of clear film (plastic wrap) and beat with the side of a rolling pin until the meat is about half its original thickness. Place in a large, shallow dish or bowl.

2 Mix together the sesame oil, garlic, coriander roots, red chillies, fish sauce and sugar in a jug (pitcher), stirring until the sugar has dissolved. Pour over the chicken and turn to coat. Cover with clear film and marinate for at least 20 minutes. Meanwhile, make the sauce.

3 Heat the vinegar in a small pan, add the sugar and stir until dissolved. Add the salt and stir until the mixture begins to thicken. Add the remaining sauce ingredients, stir well, then spoon the sauce into a serving bowl.

4 Preheat the grill (broiler) and cook the chicken for 5 minutes. Turn and baste with the marinade, then cook for 5 minutes more, or until cooked through and golden. Serve with rice and the sauce, garnished with lime wedges.

Energy 243kcal/1,022kJ; **Protein** 28g; **Carbohydrate** 17.7g, of which sugars 17.6g; **Fat** 7.1g, of which saturates 1.2g; **Cholesterol** 79mg; **Calcium** 73mg; **Fibre** 1.5g; **Sodium** 502mg.

Rosemary scented lamb

The lamb in this recipe is marinaded overnight in an oil-based mixture.

INGREDIENTS

Serves 4–8

2 x 8-chop racks of lamb, French trimmed

8 large fresh rosemary sprigs

2 garlic cloves, finely sliced

90ml/6 tbsp extra virgin olive oil

30ml/2 tbsp red wine

salt and ground pepper

1 Cut the racks into eight portions, each consisting of two linked chops, and tie a rosemary sprig to each one. Lay them in a single layer in a bowl.

2 Mix the garlic, oil and wine, and pour over the lamb. Cover and chill overnight, turning as often as possible.

3 Bring the lamb to room temperature 1 hour before cooking. Remove the lamb from the marinade. Season the meat 15 minutes before cooking.

4 Grill (broil) the chops for 5 minutes on each side. Remove from the grill (broiler), cover and rest for 10 minutes. Serve.

Energy 433kcal/1788kJ; **Protein** 23.4g; **Carbohydrate** 0g, of which sugars 0g; **Fat** 37.6g, of which saturates 16.4g; **Cholesterol** 101mg; **Calcium** 17mg; **Fibre** 0g; **Sodium** 83mg.

OILS IN ROASTED DISHES

Adding oil to roasted dishes will stop them becoming too dry in the oven. It can be used with other ingredients, or on its own to give a nice crisp finish to vegetables or meat.

Roast potatoes

A classic accompaniment to roast meat, roast potatoes are coated thoroughly in olive oil to ensure a crisp finish.

INGREDIENTS

Serves 4

1.3kg/3lb floury potatoes

90ml/6 tbsp olive oil

salt

1 Preheat the oven to 200°C/400°F/ Gas 6. Peel the potatoes and cut them into chunks.

2 Boil the potatoes in salted water for about 5 minutes, drain, return to the pan, and shake them to roughen the surfaces.

3 Put the oil into a large roasting pan and put into the hot oven to heat. Add the potatoes, coating them in the oil.

4 Return to the oven and cook for 40–50 minutes, turning once or twice, until crisp and cooked through.

Energy 484kcal/2,048kJ; **Protein** 9.4g; **Carbohydrate** 84.2g, of which sugars 2g; **Fat** 14.6g, of which saturates 5.9g; **Cholesterol** 13mg; **Calcium** 26mg; **Fibre** 5.9g; **Sodium** 29mg.

Sardines with tomatoes, thyme and purple basil

A mix of tomatoes, spices and oil infuses the fish with flavour as they roast.

INGREDIENTS

Serves 4

8 large sardines, scaled, gutted and
   thoroughly washed

6–8 fresh thyme sprigs

juice of ½ lemon

2 x 400g/14oz cans chopped tomatoes,
   drained of juice

60–75ml/4–5 tbsp olive oil

4 garlic cloves, smashed flat

5ml/1 tsp sugar

1 bunch of fresh purple basil

salt and ground black pepper

lemon wedges, to serve

1 Preheat the oven to 180°C/350°F/ Gas 4. Lay the sardines side by side in an ovenproof dish, place a sprig of thyme between each one and squeeze the lemon juice over them.

2 In a large bowl, mix together the chopped tomatoes, olive oil, garlic and sugar. Season and stir in most of the basil leaves, then pour the mixture over the sardines.

3 Bake, uncovered, for 25 minutes. Sprinkle the remaining basil leaves over the top and serve hot, with the lemon wedges.

Energy 219kcal/915kJ; **Protein** 11.7g; **Carbohydrate** 7.3g, of which sugars 7.3g; **Fat** 16.2g, of which saturates 3.1g; **Cholesterol** 0mg; **Calcium** 57mg; **Fibre** 2g; **Sodium** 78mg.

Roast shoulder of lamb with whole garlic cloves

Olive oil is drizzled over both potatoes and lamb in this recipe.

INGREDIENTS

serves 4–6

675g/1½lb waxy potatoes, peeled and cut
 into large dice
12 garlic cloves, unpeeled
45ml/3 tbsp olive oil
1 whole shoulder of lamb
salt and ground black pepper

1 Preheat the oven to 180°C/350°F/
Gas 4. Put the potatoes and garlic cloves
into a large roasting pan and season
with salt and pepper.

2 Pour over 30ml/2 tbsp of the oil and
toss the potatoes and garlic to coat.

3 Place a rack over the roasting pan,
so that it is not touching the potatoes
at all. Carefully place the shoulder
of lamb on the rack and drizzle over
the remaining oil. Season with salt
and pepper.

4 Roast the lamb and potatoes in the
oven for about 2–2½ hours, or until the
lamb is cooked through.

5 Halfway through the cooking
time, carefully take the lamb and the
rack off the roasting pan and turn
the potatoes to ensure even cooking,
replacing the lamb and the rack after
turning them.

Energy 668kcal/2775kJ; **Protein** 29.2g;
Carbohydrate 20.8g, of which sugars 1.7g; **Fat**
52.6g, of which saturates 24.1g; **Cholesterol**
113mg; **Calcium** 22mg; **Fibre** 1.8g; **Sodium** 123mg.

Aubergines in a chilli sauce

The aubergines are brushed with coconut
oil before roasting to keep them moist.

INGREDIENTS

Serves 4

4 small aubergines (eggplants), butterflied
60ml/4 tbsp coconut oil
4 shallots, finely chopped
4 garlic cloves, finely chopped
25g/1oz fresh root ginger, finely chopped
3–4 red chillies, seeded and finely chopped
400g/14oz can tomatoes, drained
5–10ml/1–2 tsp palm sugar (jaggery)
juice of 2 limes
salt
1 small bunch fresh coriander (cilantro),
 finely chopped, to garnish

1 Preheat the oven to 180°C/350°F/
Gas 4. Put the aubergines on a baking tray,
brush with 30ml/2 tbsp of the coconut oil
and bake for 40 minutes, until soft.

2 Using a mortar and pestle, grind the
shallots, garlic, ginger and chillies to a
paste. Heat the remaining 30ml/2 tbsp of
oil in a wok and stir in the spice paste and
cook for 1–2 minutes. Add the tomatoes
and sugar and cook for 3–4 minutes, then
stir in the lime juice and salt to taste.

3 Put the aubergines on to a serving dish
and spoon the sauce over them. Garnish
with the chopped coriander and serve.

Energy 100kcal/419kJ; **Protein** 2,1g;
Carbohydrate 9.4g, of which sugars 8.8g;
Fat 6.4g, of which saturates 0.9g; **Cholesterol** 0mg;
Calcium 42mg; **Fibre** 3.7g; **Sodium** 15mg.

OILS IN CAKES AND BISCUITS

In these recipes, oil is used to make a dough or batter and imparts wonderful rich flavours and added moistness to a range of sweet baking mixtures.

Olive oil biscuits

These biscuits, made with an oil-based dough, are a Portuguese favourite.

INGREDIENTS

Makes about 20

6 eggs

150ml/1/4 pint/2/3 cup olive oil

100g/3³/₄oz/generous 1/2 cup sugar

15ml/1 tbsp brandy

about 250g/9oz/2 1/4 cups plain (all-purpose)
   flour, plus extra for dusting

1 Preheat the oven to 180°C/350°F/ Gas 4. Beat the eggs with the olive oil, the sugar and brandy with an electric mixer until smooth.

2 Gradually beat in the flour on a low speed until a dough forms.

3 Fill moulds and bake for 20 to 30 minutes (depending on the size of the moulds), until golden.

4 Leave the biscuits to stand for 2 minutes and remove from the moulds.

Energy 111kcal/465kJ; **Protein** 3g;
Carbohydrate 9.7, of which sugars 0.2g; **Fat** 6.8g,
of which saturates 1.2g; **Cholesterol** 57.1mg;
Calcium 26mg; **Fibre** 0.4g; **Sodium** 21.4mg.

Apple cake

This traditional Polish cake is firm and moist, with pieces of apple peeking through the top.

INGREDIENTS

Serves 6–8

375g/13oz/3¹/₄ cups self-raising
   (self-rising) flour

3–4 large cooking apples,

10ml/2 tsp ground cinnamon

500g/1¹/₄lb/2¹/₂ cups caster
   (superfine) sugar

4 eggs, lightly beaten

250ml/8fl oz/1 cup vegetable oil

120ml/4fl oz/¹/₂ cup orange juice

10ml/2 tsp vanilla extract

2.5ml/¹/₂ tsp salt

1 Preheat the oven to 180°C/350°F/ Gas 4. Grease a 30–8cm/12–15in square cake tin (pan) and dust with a little of the flour.

2 Core and thinly slice the apples, but do not peel. Put the sliced apples in a bowl and mix with the cinnamon and 75ml/5 tbsp of the sugar.

3 In a separate bowl, beat together the eggs, remaining sugar, vegetable oil, orange juice and vanilla extract until well combined. Sift in the remaining flour and salt, then stir into the mixture.

4 Pour two-thirds of the cake mixture into the prepared tin, top with one-third of the apples, then pour over the remaining cake mixture and top with the remaining apple. Bake for 1 hour, or until golden brown.

5 Cool slightly in the tin to allow the juices to soak in. Serve cut into squares.

Energy 653kcal/2751kJ; **Protein** 7.8g;
Carbohydrate 105.4g, of which sugars 70.6g; **Fat** 25.3g, of which saturates 3.4g; **Cholesterol** 95mg; **Calcium** 215mg; **Fibre** 2.1g; **Sodium** 210mg.

Semolina cake

This is a traditional Greek cake recipe. It takes very little time to make and uses inexpensive ingredients that most Greek kitchens would have in stock.

INGREDIENTS

Serves 6–8

500g/1¼lb/2¾ cups caster (superfine) sugar

1 litre/1¾ pints/4 cups cold water

1 cinnamon stick

250ml/8fl oz/1 cup olive oil

350g/12oz/2 cups coarse semolina

50g/2oz/½ cup blanched almonds

30ml/2 tbsp pine nuts

5ml/1 tsp ground cinnamon

1 Put the sugar in a heavy pan, pour in the water and add the cinnamon stick. Bring to the boil, stirring until the sugar dissolves, then boil without stirring for about 4 minutes to make a syrup.

2 Meanwhile, heat the oil in a separate, heavy pan. When it is almost smoking, add the semolina gradually and stir constantly until it turns light brown.

3 Lower the heat, add the almonds and pine nuts, and brown together for 2–3 minutes, stirring constantly.

4 Take the semolina mixture off the heat and set aside. Remove the cinnamon stick from the hot syrup using a slotted spoon and discard it.

5 Protecting your hand with an oven glove or dish towel, carefully add the hot syrup to the semolina mixture a little at a time, stirring constantly. The mixture will probably hiss and spit at this point, so stand well away.

6 Return the pan to a gentle heat and stir until all the syrup has been absorbed and the mixture looks nice and smooth.

7 Remove the pan from the heat, cover it with a clean dish towel and let it stand for 10 minutes so that any remaining moisture is absorbed.

8 Scrape the mixture into a 20–23cm/ 8–9in round cake tin (pan), preferably fluted, and set it aside.

9 When it is cold, unmould it on to a serving platter and dust it evenly all over with the ground cinnamon. Serve in slices.

Energy 888kcal/3,731kJ; **Protein** 9.1g; **Carbohydrate** 133.1g, of which sugars 87.6g; **Fat** 39.1g, of which saturates 4.9g; **Cholesterol** 0mg; **Calcium** 75mg; **Fibre** 1.9g; **Sodium** 13mg.

Spiced apple cake

Grated apple and chopped dates give this cake a natural sweetness.

INGREDIENTS

Serves 8

225g/8oz/2 cups self-raising (self-rising) wholemeal (wholewheat) flour

5ml/1 tsp baking powder (baking soda)

10ml/2 tsp ground cinnamon

175g/6oz/1 cup chopped dates

75g/3oz/½ cup light muscovado (brown) sugar

15ml/1 tbsp pear and apple spread

120ml/4fl oz/½ cup apple juice

2 eggs

90ml/6 tbsp sunflower oil

2 eating apples, cored and grated

15ml/1 tbsp chopped walnuts

1 Preheat the oven to 180°C/350°F/Gas 4. Grease and line a 20cm/8in cake tin (pan). Sift the flour, baking powder and cinnamon into a bowl, mix in the dates and make a well in the centre.

2 Mix the sugar with the pear and apple spread in a small bowl. Gradually stir in the apple juice. Add to the dry ingredients with the eggs, oil and apples. Mix.

3 Spoon the mixture into the prepared tin, sprinkle with walnuts and bake for 1 hour, or until a skewer inserted into the cake comes out clean. Cool on a wire rack.

Energy 282kcal/1186kJ; **Protein** 4.9g; **Carbohydrate** 42.8g, of which sugars 21.3g; **Fat** 11.3g, of which saturates 1.5g; **Cholesterol** 48mg; **Calcium** 60mg; **Fibre** 1.6g; **Sodium** 22mg.

OILS IN BREADS

Olive oil is an essential ingredient in the breads of the Mediterranean region, particularly those of Greece and Italy. The addition of oil brings both moisture and flavour.

Italian olive oil bread

This classic Italian bread, known as Pugliese, is moistened and flavoured with fruity extra virgin olive oil.

INGREDIENTS

Makes one large loaf

For the biga starter

175g/6oz/1½ cups unbleached white
 bread flour

7g/¼ oz fresh yeast

90ml/6 tbsp lukewarm water

For the dough

225g/8oz/2 cups unbleached white bread
 flour, plus extra for dusting

225g/8oz/2 cups unbleached wholemeal
 (whole-wheat) bread flour

5ml/1 tsp caster (superfine) sugar

10ml/2 tsp salt

15g/½ oz fresh yeast

275ml/9fl oz/generous 1 cup lukewarm water

75ml/5 tbsp extra virgin olive oil

1 Sift the flour for the biga starter into a large bowl. Make a well in the centre. In a small bowl, cream the yeast with the water. Pour the liquid into the centre of the flour and gradually mix in the surrounding flour to form a firm dough.

2 Turn the dough out on to a floured surface and knead for 5 minutes until smooth and elastic. Return to the bowl, cover with lightly oiled clear film (plastic wrap) and leave to rise in a warm place for 8–10 hours, until the dough has risen and starts to collapse.

3 Lightly flour a baking sheet. Mix the flours, sugar and salt for the dough in a large bowl. Cream the yeast and the water in another large bowl, then stir in the biga and mix together.

4 Stir in the flour mixture a little at a time, then add the olive oil in the same way, and mix to a soft dough. Turn out on to a floured surface and knead for 8–10 minutes until smooth and elastic. Place in a lightly oiled bowl, cover with lightly oiled clear film and leave to rise, in a warm place, for 1–1½ hours, or until doubled in bulk.

5 Turn out on to a lightly floured surface and knock back (punch down). Gently pull out the edges and fold under to make a round. Transfer to the prepared baking sheet, cover with lightly oiled clear film and leave in a warm place, for 1–1½ hours, until doubled in size.

6 Meanwhile, preheat the oven to 230°C/450°F/Gas 8. Lightly dust the loaf with flour and bake for 15 minutes. Reduce the oven to 200°C/400°F/Gas 6 and bake for 20 minutes more, until the loaf sounds hollow when tapped.

Energy 2502kcal/10567kJ; **Protein** 72g; **Carbohydrate** 430.4g, of which sugars 11.8g; **Fat** 66.7g, of which saturates 9.5g; **Cholesterol** 0mg; **Calcium** 468mg; **Fibre** 43g; **Sodium** 3949mg.

Polenta and pepper bread

This bread is delicious when drizzled with a little olive oil.

INGREDIENTS

Makes 2 loaves

175g/6oz/1½ cups polenta

5ml/1 tsp salt

350g/12oz/3 cups unbleached strong plain
 flour, plus extra for dusting

5ml/1 tsp sugar

7g/¼oz sachet easy-blend dried yeast

1 red (bell) pepper, roasted, peeled and diced

15ml/1 tbsp olive oil

1 Mix the polenta, salt, flour, sugar and yeast in a bowl. Stir in the pepper until it is evenly distributed, then make a well in the centre of the mixture. Grease two loaf tins.

2 Add 300ml/½ pint/1¼ cups warm water and the olive oil and mix to a soft dough. Knead for 10 minutes until smooth and elastic.

3 Place in an oiled bowl, cover with oiled clear film (plastic wrap) and leave to rise in a warm place for 1 hour until doubled. Knock back the dough, knead lightly, then divide in two.

4 Shape each piece into an oblong and place in the tins. Cover with oiled clear film and leave to rise for 45 minutes. Preheat the oven to 220°C/ 425°F/Gas 7.

5 Bake for 30 minutes until golden. Leave for 5 minutes, then cool on a wire rack.

Energy 1994kcal/8427kJ; **Protein** 50.5g; **Carbohydrate** 366.9g, of which sugars 7.1g; **Fat** 44.7g, of which saturates 15.1g; **Cholesterol** 53mg; **Calcium** 1085mg; **Fibre** 14.9g; **Sodium** 2337mg.

INDEX